LET'S PARTY!™

HOW TO succeed in PARTY PLAN

Strategies For Maximizing Your Business.
Setting Your Sights For Higher Earnings.
Increasing Productivity.
Increasing Sales and Recruiting.
Seeing More People.

by Jan Ruhe

BOOKS BY JAN RUHE

Fire Up!
MLM Nuts $ Bolts
The Lady of the Rings
The Rhino Spirit
Let's Party!
The Master Presentation Guide

BOOKS COAUTHORED BY JAN RUHE

True Leadership
Go Diamond

LET'S PARTY!™

ISBN 0-9702667-6-6
LCCN: 2004090640

Jan Ruhe
www.janruhe.com

Cover Design by David Anselmo.

This Edition Published by
Bids Supplies Ltd
Cardiff
E Mail - bids4agents@aol.com

Dedication

To all who have hosted a Home Party.
You are the lifeblood of our business.

To my children, *Clayton, Ashley* and *Sarah*,
who were my reasons for building
a Network Marketing business through
the Party Plan method.

To my *Nana*, for giving me the initial
investment to buy that first kit of products.

And to the thousands of Network Marketers who
have been or are my students world wide.

TABLE OF CONTENTS

Rave Reviews for *Let's Party*

"It is exciting and fun when we get a group of people together to share the benefits of our products and opportunity. We started our Network Marketing business after attending a party and it has completely changed our lives. As friends and students of Jan Ruhe for years we have learned so much from her wisdom. Let's Party! is a definite must read."
-Chris and Alan Goldsbrough
Forever Living Products, England

"I conducted my first Home Party 36 years ago, and what is amazing is that we still use this technique today. When you get 12-24 people at a Party, some will buy your products and some will join to sell, and some just spread the good word."
-Ruth Lemire
Pre-Paid Legal Services Inc., USA

"Let's Party is the right tool for every Party Plan business. Gather all the wisdom and knowledge from Jan Ruhe she is the Party Plan expert. After all, we get paid to PARTY!"
-Cathy Barber
The Pampered Chef, Canada

"Great scripts, terrific skills, hands-on experience from a Top Distributor! I have been fortunate to have been coached by Jan Ruhe for over a decade. Get this book, devour it, then teach others to make magic with Party Plan. Watch your business explode!"
-Teri McClure Dinnius
Discovery Toys, USA

"In my 18 years of Network Marketing full-time, I feel the reason Party Plans are growing so much is because it takes your business to another level by keeping it fun, simple, easy and magical."
-Jeff and Tracy Weisberg
New Vision, USA

"At last! A book about Party Plan from the Diva of Network Marketing herself, Jan Ruhe! Having been my friend and mentor, Jan's teachings are the major reason for my success and with this book you can use her wisdom and experience to get there too! My team will be clambering to add this latest jewel to their library of 'gotta-have' Jan Ruhe books!"
-Sherry Shadab
Southern Living At Home, USA

"The Party Plan method of sales has worked for me. Thanks to leaders like Jan Ruhe who still walk and talk what they write. Putting into action the advice in her books, I have risen to the top of my company. This book is filled to the brim with ideas that can help you help yourself go to the top of your compensation plan. Read these ideas, act on these ideas, train these ideas and share these ideas."
-Janet Wakeland
Stampin' UP!, USA

"Want a straight forward guide to help you climb to the top in Party Plan? Let's Party gives you the practical, ready to implement ideas you need. Jan Ruhe shares her wealth of experience in Party Plan to benefit you as you become a top distributor. This book is priceless!"
-Nancy Ann Wartman
Usborne Books, USA

Introduction

Here is a book that will help you master Party Plan. It will nourish you with exciting ideas for packing your life with more abundance and prosperity than you ever dreamed possible!

While writing this book, I hoped that you would not think that Party Plan is complicated because there is so much information herein. I discovered that over 20 years is a lot of years to gather ideas and wisdom, and I wanted to put every idea I could think of in this book to help you succeed.

The Party Plan method of selling, recruiting and teaching others to do the same is a well-respected profession. I have made millions, as many others have, by realizing that we are merely resellers of products owned by a corporation. The corporation has warehouses full of products and the job of the distributor is to move product out of those warehouses. You start with a small investment and can make a fortune. The information contained in this book is not theory, it is fact.

> *"Believe nothing, no matter where you read it, or who said it, no matter if I have said it, unless it agrees with your own reason and your own common sense."*
> -Buddha

Who am I to write this book? Who am I to coach you or guide you? Read my story in the upcoming pages so that you will trust that I have done that which I am going to share with you. I have not quit Network Marketing to become a trainer to tell you *how to* do the business. If Network Marketing is so great, why would I quit? Why would I want to learn from someone who quit or *"retired"* at an early age to become a trainer? Why would I let anyone teach me that was not going for greatness? I wouldn't. I will only share with you powerful ideas that I have tried myself and know that work.

Many trainers will tell you they got to the top by talent, hard work or luck. I discovered years ago that I needed systems, scripts and techniques. I had raw enthusiasm when I started my climb to the top. It did not take long to realize that for the business to get to the level I wanted it to, and for me to continue to spend quality time loving my children and to reach my goal of being a multi-millionaire, that I would have to learn strategies that would help me change myself into the person I wanted to become.

I searched the world for information and in many cases found no one who had blazed a trail to follow. So, I began to blaze one myself. I had no idea that others would come after me and want to know my path. After discovering what not to do and figuring out how to succeed massively in Party Plan, I decided to write this book to help those of you, who are serious about being the best you can be in Party Plan, to get to the top of your Pay Plan.

The first step to being credible in anything is experience. After over 2 decades, I still don't know it all. I know that if you really want to make this work, wild lions won't stop you! So it's time to say:

Let's Party!

The top bananas get the most light.

Section 1

My Story....

My Story

In 1979, I was a stay at home mother of 2 young children. My husband, at the time, had a job but we found that there was always too much month at the end of the money. He went to work, and I played with the children. I settled for a mediocre lifestyle. I shrank my dreams to match his income. **Don't use expecting a baby as an excuse:** Baby number 3, Ashley was on the way.

Have a reason *Why* you want to succeed: I wanted to send my 4 year old Sarah to private school. The school had a mission...*a child is not a vessel to be filled but a lamp to be lighted.* I loved that mission. My **why** was my children and our future.

What happened? I began to dream. My husband didn't.

Don't you hate these words? I don't know when it happened but I began to **HATE** the words: "*We can't afford it; when we can afford it; practical; budget; functional; get by...*" My children were invited to play at homes with playmates whose parents owned airplanes, yachts, limos, swimming pools and had fresh flowers in their houses. I saw that lifestyle and wanted it for my children. I began to dream bigger. *Why couldn't we live like that?* My husband began to try to constantly control what I did and what I thought. He wasn't growing. I was growing and miserable. I was changing.

People change as life unfolds: By the fall of 1979, I realized that if we were going to have enough money to get a better lifestyle, then it was up to me. I would have to earn the money.

My Point: For things to change in your life you have to change. Say to yourself: "*If it's going to be, it's up to me.*"

Party Plan got my attention: I started paying attention to home based businesses wondering what they were all about. My desires were really uncomplicated. I was willing to have Home Parties so I could make enough money to achieve just a few goals. *Have you ever woken up and observed something that has been around you for years, but you somehow had not noticed it?*

Next: Almost overnight, I started paying attention to the fact that there were people selling products out of their homes, making money and driving cars they had earned. No one ever asked me to join them or I probably would have. I wondered if I could succeed in building a business out of my home. I wanted to be recruited, be needed, to belong and to make some extra money and no one even tried to recruit me.

My point: Do not take for granted that your friends or acquaintances would not want to join you. Share the opportunity with everyone.

Ask everyone: I decided that selling something at home was probably not for me as no one thought I could succeed at it. I forgot about it and just shrunk my dreams.

Fate takes a turn: November, 1979, I was invited to a Home Party. Perhaps this could be my future career? I was excited!

The Party: Ava showed us the products, answered our questions, and took our orders. She gave a short, fun, easy to duplicate presentation. As she talked, I could barely contain my excitement. **This was it!** I felt this way: *"I can do this! I can set up some products and become a reseller of products and make some money AND stay home with my babies! PERFECT!"* My heart was pounding! I had a dream! I found my passion! To work from home while raising my children. I was ready and willing. I was fired up!

My point: You want your guests to feel that exact way at your Parties. You never know who is in your audience. Don't miss recruiting someone like me. Ask everyone you meet to join you.

Here is what happened next...

Total Disappointment: Alas, at the end of the Party, Ava did not mention joining her nor scheduling any Parties. I knew I had to speak up and I said: "*I want ALL of your products but can only afford $40 to spend today. I want to schedule a Party so I can get some toys for FREE*!"

My point: Make everyone at your Party desire to own all or many of your products.

I was ready: I just blurted it out! I was going to have my first Home Party! I had never held a Home Party! I was sincerely excited!

Next: Ava said she was booked for the rest of the year and had no time to schedule a Party with me.

My Point: Schedule your calendar full of Home Parties. What she didn't know and neither did I was that at that very moment, she changed my life. I became persistent. Me, the housewife with little self-esteem. I wanted to do what she did. Now!

Give out business cards: Ava gave me her business card and said: "*Call me in early 1980 to schedule a Party. I am booked by mid January for the year*." From November to January, every day I thought about joining to sell through Party Plan.

Next: At home I shared with my husband how excited I was and about possibly hosting a Party. I told him about what I had ordered, and he told me to *cancel my order*. He said we didn't have the money to invest in those toys. I cancelled the order and was devastated. I was so disappointed. Forget about my desires and dreams. No money. No dreams. Settle, don't rock the boat.

My point: You can always justify having less, and spending less. But you can always choose to dream.

The New Year! A new DECADE! By January of 1980, I called Ava to get on her schedule to have a Party as the Host.

Dreams do wake up: Inside, I was thrilled with the possibilities of earning my own money. No longer would I have to justify what I was spending. I was sick and tired of that life.

My point: When you get sick and tired of being sick and tired, you will make changes in your life.

New beginnings: I called Ava on January 1, 1980. There was no answer. There were no answering machines at the time. I would keep trying. I called her January 2, 3, 4, 5, and still no answer. I was mega interested in doing what *she was doing. I wanted to get going! I was so excited!*

My point: You never know who will be thinking about joining you a month or two later. Be accessible. Follow up. Don't miss one recruit.

I had found my passion: I was passionately eager and kept calling Ava until I finally reached her. She told me that she was busy and could I call her back? I explained to her my interest but she was too busy to listen. I called her back the first part of February and she had no time for me. In desperation, I finally called her back March 1st and blurted out, ***"I WANT TO SELL THESE TOYS!"***

She said: "*I have quit. I would appreciate it if you would not call me again! You are annoying me!*" Brutal. I was crushed. I barely had any self-esteem and could not believe it. I was devastated.

Next: I asked her how I could get a kit of the products. She gave me Mary's phone number. When I called Mary she told me that *she was* thinking of quitting. I told her that I wanted to join and *how could I get a kit?* She asked me to come to her office the next day to pick up a contract for me to sign to buy a kit of products. OH NO! A *contract* to sign.

My point: Watch your words. A *contract*? I picked up the contract, and discussed buying the kit with my husband. He said we didn't have the money for the kit. We could not afford the $250 to buy the kit of products. Quit dreaming? Nope. I signed the *contract*. A better word would have been *"paperwork"*.

When you truly want the money to join Network Marketing you will find it: Money is not ever *the issue*. The issue is the depth of your desire to find the money to get involved. The kit is an investment into your future.

Not to be denied: I called my grandmother and asked to borrow the money for the kit. She said: "*Honey, I will stake a claim in your future, come and get a check for $250 anytime*!"

My point: If you really want to invest in a product kit, you will find a way. You will find the money. Not having any money is *not an excuse*.

With a gratitude attitude: March 8, 1980. With the contract and check for the kit in hand, I took them to Mary's office. Mary told me my kit would arrive in 2 weeks, to go ahead and schedule a Party for 2 weeks later. And I did.

Next: Mary came to my home, sat in our living room and trained me for 15 minutes explaining some of the products. She never mentioned recruiting or training others to do the same.

My point: Don't over-analyze to get started.

1980-1984
The Formulative and Concentration Years

Ready to take on the world: I was ready to present these products at my upcoming Party! I called Mary at least 100 times to ask her questions. I had a zillion questions. She was uninterested in helping me and finally, she said she was quitting and would I not call her anymore. Right before my first Party! How could I do this on my own? I got an attitude, I would just do it. I would do fine on my own.

I would figure it out!

Here is what I did: When the kit arrived, my children, Sarah (4), Clayton (2) and I played with the toys. We loved all of the products. I was excited to have my own business! I got to know the products by playing with them.

My point: Get familiar with your products. Get excited about your products. Get fired up!

Let's Party!

My First Home Party

The big night came for my first Party with 20 guests. I arrived an hour early, took **one hour** to set up the products and was quite nervous. I had never spoken to a group in my life. The guests arrived and I gave the most fantastic presentation you can imagine, so I thought. Everyone loved the products, I did not recruit anyone and did not schedule a future Party. BUT, I sold a whopping $75 to TWENTY people! I was thrilled, someone bought *something* from me. From that night on, I was *fired up for the remainder of my career, forever.*

My point: You want your recruits to be *fired up* from their first Party onward! Don't give up, don't give in, try again and again. Learn while you earn.

Here is how: Become a student of Party Plan. Book by book, seminar by seminar, Party by Party, you will learn what to do differently to increase sales, recruiting and your income. Study Party Plan.

Ten years later...a woman called me and joined my team, she had moved to Florida and had thought about joining me that long...she had been at my first Party. So, after all, *I did get a recruit a my first Party.*

1985-1995
The Momentum Years

Fast Forward 20+ Years

I went through a divorce, was a single mother for 5 years, and married Bill Ruhe in 1990. We moved from Texas to Colorado and built our dream home. I wrote 7 books, today in many languages. I am a Network Marketing trainer worldwide, have friends around the world and have college educated all three of my children. By the end of 2003, I had over 10,000 distributors in the USA. Over 50% of the entire company was in my successline.

Tough times never last, but tough people do: No situation slowed me down.

My point: Hold a lot of Parties to move products and *show the way* for others to do the same.

I built my business one Party at a time.

1996-2000
The Stability Years

The result: I got the lifestyle. You can get it too!

My point: Be willing to work to achieve your dreams. If it was easy to get to the top, everyone would be there.

The lifestyle: The lifestyle has been fabulous. The children and I survived *solely* on my income from my Party Plan business.

My point: If you want something badly enough, you will get it. If you are willing to work to get it, you *must* succeed. The only way to not succeed is to quit. You must work for success, be assured it's there. If the promise is clear, the how to get it will become easy.

For the distributor who has built their organization around contribution, the stability stage can provide a financial freedom and lifestyle second to none.

Go for the Lifestyle

If you want to live with opulence, have experiences that are beyond the ordinary, escape to tropical havens, discover a world that fills your expectations and fulfills your imagination, enjoy an array of live entertainment, have the world's finest creature comforts, shop in designer boutiques, stay at spas that attend to every concern, enjoy life that is nothing short of divine, have friends worldwide, enjoy heritage still to be found among buildings, the arts, the smells, the traditions, have a quiet rest yachting, carry the black American Express credit card, enjoy the glitz of Monaco and Las Vegas, see all of Europe, have a jewelry box overflowing with diamonds, have wonderful children, a loving husband, enjoy priceless privacy and security, dine at extravagant restaurants, consummate social and recreational pleasures, enjoy the beautiful beaches along the oceans of the world, enjoy personal pampering and get more kicks out of life than you ever dreamed possible... Start from wherever you are right now and decide to go to the top of Network Marketing. It is a valid and respected profession today. Start your climb out of mediocrity to the top, today.

Here is the exciting news: If I did it...

so can you!

Nervous About Speaking In Front Of A Group

The best way to get over the fright or fear of speaking in front of people is to stop thinking about yourself and start thinking about what you have to offer others. Work hard to get over being worried to speak in front of others.

Here is how: When nervous, write down key words that you want to make sure you speak about and put them on card stock and read them. You don't have to be a performer. You are sharing a product and opportunity. Move your arms to help the jitters depart sooner.

Remember: If the butterflies are all flying in formation in your stomach, you are going to do just fine.

Note: Yard by yard is hard, inch by inch it's a cinch, mile by mile, you will arrive in style with a smile.

"LEARN TO LOVE TO PARTY"
-David Anselmo

Realize How Your Guests And Hosts Really Feel

Don't put so much fear into presenting. When you think to yourself *"I'm scared, I'm nervous, I am going to pass out!"* Me. Me. Me... Don't lose sight of your Hosts and guests. In fact, your Hosts and guests may be more scared than you. It's important to know the following 3 things about your Hosts and audience...

1. The Host and guests want you to succeed: By showing up, the Host and guests give you a tremendous vote of confidence. They don't want to spend their time to come and hear you fail. They want your presentation to be a success. When your presentation is terrific, your Hosts and guests feel that they made the right choice in attending the Party.

2. You have knowledge that the Host and guests want: You were asked to hold the Party for a reason. It's because you have information that the guests desires. You are the expert. You have information that your guests are interested in. Only you can provide your own unique insights. No one else knows your information like you do.

3. The audience doesn't know that you are afraid: Often, your guests won't even detect that you are anxious.

Imagine yourself being the top producer in your company because you have mastered Party Plan

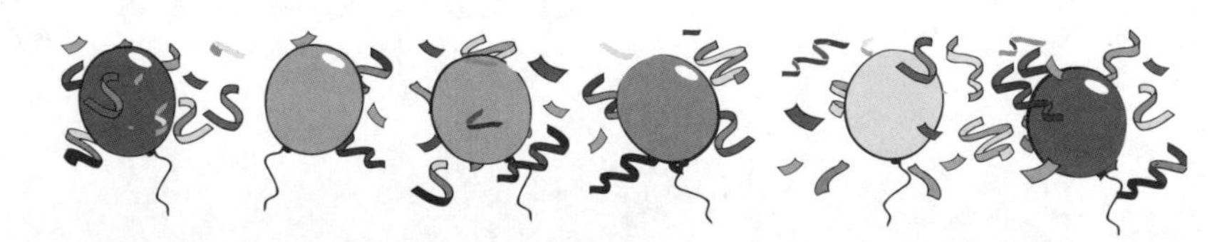

Section 2

To Begin, Be Motivated From Within....

Life Prepares Us For Party Plan

Every time we convince someone about anything, where to go, what to buy or even to get married, we are SELLING. When people react negatively to the idea of being in sales they are probably relating to some pushy sales person they had met previously who offended them. In absolute contrast, in Party Plan, when you are sharing with someone about the things that do good and have a purpose, you are actually helping, serving and assisting people in making a decision that you feel is a good one for them. Everyone "*sells*" when asking for decisions during every day communication. Selling is a natural skill. Be proud to be in Sales.

Take Urgent Action

The more Parties you do and the more people you teach to do the same, the quicker you will achieve your goals. Start where you are. Hurry, take urgent action and start now. You can't stroll to a goal.

An Amazing Future Awaits You

If you choose to do nothing and not try Party Plan, that is okay, *nothing* will change in your life and everything will stay the same. You checked it out, that's all. *BUT, if you decide to start in Party Plan and you do not quit, you can have the most amazing future that you can imagine.* The choice is yours... Explore Party Plan, it is a way out of debt and it's a way to have a dazzling future. For things to change, you must change. It's your turn to shine.

THE D-V-S-A SUCCESS SYSTEM

If you have a strong desire and a vision that you *will achieve*, you will NOT waste your life time. Decide what strategies you need to take action so that you will achieve your goal. Work on the vision of the outcome of what you want to have, do, and be in life. Then get a strategy and go into action.

I AM GOING TO TAKE YOU ON A MAGIC CARPET RIDE AND SHOW YOU THINGS YOU HAVE NEVER SEEN BEFORE, YOU CAN PAY ATTENTION, TAKE ACTION OR BUY SOME DRAPES TO MATCH IT AND PUT IT ON THE FLOOR!

Now Is The BEST Time To Be In Party Plan

Home Parties Are ONE Way

Parties are not *the only* way to do Network Marketing. It is just **one** way. And I believe it is the best way. You can choose to build the business this way. When you schedule 52 Parties a year, at other people's homes and give presentations, you will realize that this method works. You don't have to know *how to do Party Plan* when you start. Don't make it complicated. Seek out those who have great presentation skills, copy them, study presentation skills, learn about your products/opportunity and make a fortune. **My point:** Learn while you earn. There is so much information in this book that if you put it into action, success will be yours.

The Deeper Meaning Of Desire To Succeed

To begin you must have a deep belief of more than just the possibilities that you might succeed, **you need *sincere* desire**. **Why?** If you have desire and stickability, and stick around to see the payoff of your efforts, there is no way you will not succeed. Without massive desire, you are doomed.

The Basis For All Success Is Desire

Sincerely *WANT* to succeed and want to overcome any and all stumbling blocks to any challenges that you have in Party Plan. Be willing to not make excuses and to take action. Forever.

The Fire Of Desire

Your activity will either promote you or expose you. It all starts with the fire of desire. Either you have it, or you don't. Get the fire! Fire up! It starts today!

Be Eager To Succeed

When you are serious, you will discover that life time is valuable. It's all about ***lifetime.*** You will be eager to succeed and that eagerness will drive you to take massive action. Be eager to succeed. Now! **My point:** See what you can accomplish in a short amount of time, say 3 to 5 years. It takes time to grow a Party Plan business. Success in Party Plan is not overnight. It's not about holding 2-3 Parties, recruiting 5-10 people and sitting back to see what happens. It's about being eager to press on until you reach your goal.

Times Have Changed

We have experienced many changes in the world. We all experienced the agony of 9-11, terrorist alerts, more security worldwide at airports, fear and countless other life lessons that our predecessors did not encounter or have to adjust to. Now, more than ever, cocooning is a way of life. Today, we bring food, workout equipment, movies, DVD's, meetings, and almost every product you can imagine into the home.

Belonging And Congregating Are Important

People still congregate at churches, sporting events, school events, country clubs, athletic clubs, malls, pubs, bars, etc. Families live miles apart now and today call "*getting together*" reunions.

The need for gathering, belonging, congregating, the breaking of bread, which are huge human needs, has not changed.

Now is THE time to be in Party Plan!

Here is why Parties work ...

The bottom line

Parties Are FUN And Save Time!

Be A Human Being, Not A Human Doing

Humans ***want*** to get together, to entertain, to connect, to belong, to socialize, to be needed, to be included, and to be invited. Now is *THE time* in Network Marketing to be in Party Plan. The timing has *never* been better! Home Parties are a valid, successful, inexpensive way of getting people together to congregate, to be together, to shop, to give outstanding customer service, to look at products, invest in them and to have an enjoyable experience.

You are at the right place at the right time.

Prepare To Get *Fired Up*!

Once you start scheduling Parties from Parties and learn how to do a Party a week, do the math, you will see more people. The more people you share your product and opportunity with the more will join you. In fact, you will get *so fired up, you won't be able to help but schedule Parties.*

The Common Denominator Of Instant Success

Do you know what the common denominator of instant success is? It is having an enthusiastic attitude. It is a proven fact that the most successful distributors are those who develop and maintain an enthusiastic attitude. Enthusiasm is the most powerful force you have working for you. Others will see that you are happy and prosperous, and they will want to join you.

Enthusiasm Paves The Way To The Top

Enthusiasm: glows, radiates, permeates and captures the interest of everyone.
Enthusiasm: adds an extra spark to make you wake up and live.
Enthusiasm: produces a confidence that cries to the world: *"I've got what it takes,"* without your uttering a word.
Enthusiasm: spreads like a prairie fire on a windy day igniting everyone with the fire of desire.
Enthusiasm: says, *"I am sold myself."*
Enthusiasm: shouts, *"I love what I do!"*

Focus On Results

The strategy is clear. Eliminate, as much as possible, those things you do during the day that are not income producing. Regardless of whether you are selling a product that requires you to make calls or follow up with clients, or involves no repeat sales, time is measured against your sales results. Results are the name of the game. Produce results. Results stacked upon results brings you an incredible future.

It Starts Today!

Want Big Checks?

Your check is measured by how many products you can move out of the company warehouse. The more products you move, the more valuable you are. You have only two choices on how to move product.

Choice #1: You can move it by yourself, OR
Choice #2: You can recruit others to do the same. The key to success in Party Plan is in thousands of distributors each selling a little bit. THOUSANDS of people each doing a little bit.

Would you rather make 40% on your own efforts or 3% on the efforts of thousands?

Next: Do the math. The money in Party Plan comes from bringing in people who will move product and teaching others to do the same. It's not hard. It's very uncomplicated. It's simply a numbers game. The more products you move the more you earn.

Get Some Training Before You Start Out On Your Path To The Top

It's CLEAR to your Host and guests if you are prepared and trained or not. You don't need a lot of training. *But* you do need to know how to easily explain how to join you and get started at the Party if someone wishes to join you right then. Don't think you need to wait to recruit at Parties until you "*figure it all out*." Start recruiting aggressively from your first Party. Don't miss a potential star because of your hesitation. Take your cell phone with you and your Upline's phone number. If you need some advice during or after your presentation call and check on information to help your guests.

Every successful person has something to prove

What To Say When People Ask You What You Do

- **I am a professional Party Planner for (company)**
- **I am a professional recruiter for (company)**
- **I bring attention to people, make them famous, successful and wealthy, but not necessarily in that order.**

SW, SW, SW...SW

Some will schedule Parties with you,
Some won't, So what...
Next...
Someone is waiting.

> **"WHEN THE STUDENT IS READY, THE TEACHER APPEARS."**
> -Tom Hopkins

Stage	LifeTime	Party Plan
Formulative	0-6 yrs.	1-4 wks.
Concentration	6-20 yrs	1-2 yrs.
Momentum	20-50 yrs	3-5 yrs.
Stability	50+ yrs.	Financial Independence

The Natural Progression Of Party Plan

There are many highs and lows, slows and goes in Party Plan. Stock markets, wars, terror alerts, holidays, family situations, meetings, vacations, sales trends, competition, health and so many other factors affect how we do our business.

As you learn about ideas and strategies to grow a Party Plan business you will progress in personal growth and development by reading, attending conferences, meetings, seminars, reading, studying where you are weak and staying focused. You move toward fulfillment and satisfaction. It is natural to work. Don't like the idea of an 8-5 job? A boss ? Or, alarm clocks? Want to be in control of your destiny, to be independent, to form your own successlines, have your own meetings, and try your wings of leadership? The natural progression is to help distributors to be independent. You know that you have a successful business when you can leave it for 2 months and it runs fine without you.

Proceed one step at a time, lay a solid foundation and do not be easily discouraged. The following information shows the natural stages of progression and how they relate to a lifetime, and a Party Plan career. The associated ages and time periods are only approximate.

The Formulative Stage:

This is the shortest period, but it's the most critical since it is when you chart your path to the top. You formulate attitudes, beliefs, habits, actions, purposes, passions and plans. You begin to search for more information, ideas, excitement, and for people who are like minded who want what you want.

The Concentration Stage:

This can be 6 months of concentrated effort to several years at a slower pace. This is when you are building your foundation for your future. Get a plan during this stage and go to work building your business. You will not be denied. You focus. Big time.

The Momentum Stage:

Once a properly built successline reaches a certain size, it seems to explode. You realize that your successline is growing by leaps and bounds and that the growth seems to be effortless. That's momentum. The key is that the longer you stay in The Concentration Stage, the longer The Momentum Stage will last. It's exhilarating. Enjoy every minute of these years. They are so much fun!

The Stability Stage:

If you built your Party Plan business right, by going wide, your leaders will be strong and will run your business. You will have an extremely stable business.

Now Is The Time In Life To Say *Let's Party!*

The day of congregating on the front porch, community centers, chatting at the barber shop, sitting at a diner and chatting the day away, customer service in most stores, and of having someone really want to help you invest in something you desire, is long gone. The day of having polite people wait on you and of taking the time to shop leisurely for hours, is gone. The time of feeling completely safe in our world is gone. Today rarely do you hear of anyone having a Party of any kind. Many Network Marketing companies have Launches, Business Builders meetings, Workshops and call getting together anything BUT a Party. Parties are fun. Be proud to be the distributor who presents products at a Party. In fact, *love it*. Why not be the one to start up the idea of Parties in your area? Now is the time to say, *Let's Party!* If you do, you will have little to no competition. People want to Party!

Be yourself, nobody plays the part better

It's In Black And White

There are only excuses why we fail or reasons why we succeed. Overcome your hesitations and doubts and go for greatness. The world is full of those who won't. Be the one who says,

"Let's Party!"

At first, in Party Plan you do a lot and make very little, but later you do very little and make a lot.

4 Easy Steps To Success In Party Plan

 # 1. Love the product.

 # 2. Sell the product.

 # 3. Sell the opportunity.

 # 4. Teach others to do the same.

For things to change,
you must change.
For things to get better
You must get better.

-Jim Rohn

Breaking Into The Party Plan Business

Every distributor who wants to make big money, who wants to earn the most money in Party Plan, has everything in their favor today. Today is the greatest opportunity for high-volume selling our world has ever seen. People have never had so much money to spend nor been so anxious to spend it. Technology is expanding at the speed of light. The demand for goods, services and great customer service, and bringing products into the home is rising spectacularly. No success comes easy. No one will set you at the top of Party Plan, you have to work at it and make it happen, and you can. The sad reality is so few do. Distributors jump from company to company, think the grass is greener on the other side, think their new Upline will help them more and on it goes. I have been in the business for over 2 decades in this industry and have a suggestion for those of you who are coachable. Find ONE company, stick with it and GET TO THE TOP. Oh yes, you will be tempted and asked to join other companies. Breaking into Party Plan is easy if you stick with one company. Remember the grass has to be mowed on both sides.

Expect Change

Nothing stays the same for long. Certainly nothing ever stays the same forever. All we can count on is that change is happening every day in every way. Expect it, prepare for it. Every 5 years, there will be upheaval in life. It's just the way life works.

The Big Carrot

Do you want time freedom to be successful, to enjoy an incredible lifestyle, travel, train, speak, have successful friends, money and make a difference? Well, if you do, that's the Big Carrot. Your travel expenses will be tax deductible and you will get paid for doing something that is both enjoyable and rewarding. Your success will be much more than money. You will have unlimited opportunities for personal growth, contribution and empowerment of others. You can throw away your alarm clock and have the time freedom to do whatever you want whenever you want. To get the Big Carrot, you have to operate within a structure that keeps your life on track, the track of giving. Not giving money, but giving your time, energy, effort, significance, recognition for years. If you want to be empowering and powerful in our culture, commit to excellence in Party Plan.

A fabulous future awaits you.

Transfer regret into

get, get, get!

There is a day that you get into Network Marketing, but nothing happens until the day Network Marketing gets inside of you.
Until you totally decide to succeed in Party Plan, you will be hesitant and you will struggle. But, the day you decide to go to the top, and you are serious, wild horses can't stop you.
You will pretend you are being chased by a lion and you won't stop until you are at the top. Period.
It's just that simple. No situation and no disappointment will devastate you.
You will be, no doubt, unstoppable.
Make today the day that you decide to decide to say... Let's Party!

Don't let your convictions become your restrictions

Today's Buyers Have A Buying Motive

No sale is ever made unless the buyer has a specific buying motive. This infallible rule: *behind every sale exists a reason to buy.* Knowing these motives can be your ticket to the top. Motives vary from guest to guest. One has a different motive from another for buying the identical product. The same guest may have different motives at different times for buying the same product. Study buying motives. Get these ingrained in your thoughts as you prospect, schedule Parties, recruit and train others to do the same.

The 10 Main Buying Motives

Ten common buying motives account for most recruits and sales. Here they are:

1. **Desire for wealth.**
2. **Desire for health.**
3. **Desire for admiration from others.**
4. **Desire for gratification of some appetite.**
5. **Desire for amusement.**
6. **Desire for safety of self or dependents.**
7. **Desire for utility or use value.**
8. **Desire for self improvement.**
9. **Desire for saving of time, trouble or worry.**
10. **Desire for comfort.**

A specific product usually appeals to only one, or a few, of the 10 reasons to buy. When you answer the question "*Which buying motive (or motives) does my product or opportunity satisfy*?" Then formulate a successful presentation around your product's benefits that best satisfy those motives.

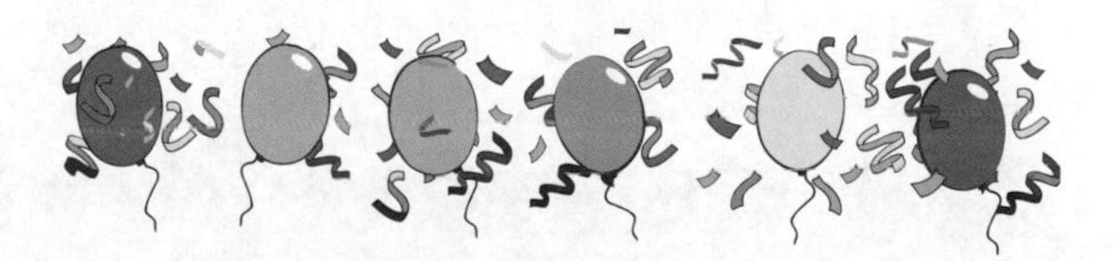

Prepare To Adjust

Stay aware of your need to prepare for change. As your business grows, you must add, delete, readjust, redirect, and redefine your goals. As you build a team of distributors, you will be holding trainings and meetings and will have to adjust when you are available to do Home Parties.

Help Distributors Become Independent Leaders

It's a great idea to take new distributors with you to watch how you do the Party. The idea is to build INDEPENDENT distributors so that they can have the confidence to do the Party without your help. If you have a group of distributors dependent on you, you are NOT a top distributor in Network Marketing. You want your successline to be independent of you. Give guidance and on going training, but not to the point that you can't do your own personal business. Managing a huge Network Marketing business is not difficult. With cell phones, palm pilots, PC's, voice mail, and technology increasing with great speed, you can make calls on the way to your Parties and on the way home. You can do it all, you can be a great parent AND build your income by holding Parties at the same time.

Time = Money

You can earn an incredible income by putting the correct value on your time and never forgetting how valuable it is. If you want to earn a bigger paycheck and not just a playcheck, *you must be* sharply aware of the money value of each hour of your working day. Don't waste time being unproductive.

Home Parties Save Time

If you want to make a lot of money... **do this**...get more value out of each of your working hours. It takes the same time, effort, and attention to talk to one person at a time as it does to do a Party, and talk to many.

Place Value On Your Time

Fix the value on your time in relation to what you want to earn and what you are willing to sacrifice to achieve your goals. Then earn it by working with prospects, customers and distributors you recruit whose productivity can yield you earnings commensurate with your time value.

A Philosophy About Time That Has Served Me Well

Lead me, follow me,

or get out of my way.

How Much Time Will You Work Per Week?

Time counts if you are going to make money. Your first goal is to find and dedicate just 10 hours a week to your Party Plan business. Have you heard: "*I don't have any time, mothering my one child is a full time job!*" Clearly, being a parent can be overwhelming. I mothered 3 young children and still found the time to hold Parties. So can you. Success is a choice.

My point: Set an initial goal. Be prepared to adjust it and what you are doing with your time as your business grows. Your goals will change.

Be consistently insistent

Figure Time Value/Hour

Calculate the money value of your time:
1. How much do you want to earn a year; and
2. There are 1952 working hours in a year of 244 working days (take away weekends, vacations, illness, and holidays).
Next: Divide your earnings goal by 1952 hours and you have it. Here are the figures for some attainable goals:

CHART #1

Earnings goal per year = Value of an hour

Earnings goal per year	Value of an hour
$10,000=	$ 5.10
$20,000=	$10.25
$25,000=	$12.80
$30,000=	$15.35
$40,000=	$20.50
$50,000=	$25.60
$60,000=	$30.74
$70,000=	$35.86
$80,000=	$40.98
$90,000=	$46.10
$100,000=	$51.22

CHART #2

Earnings goal per year = Value of an hour spent in actual Home Party

Earnings goal per year	Value of an hour spent in actual Home Party
$10,000=	$1,000
$20,000=	$2,000
$30,000=	$3,000
$40,000=	$4,000
$50,000=	$5,000
$60,000=	$6,000
$70,000=	$7,000
$80,000=	$8,000
$90,000=	$9,000
$100,000=	$10,000

Simple Math Can Bring You Riches

Now that you know how much your time is worth, you can see the importance of using your time doing Parties. Offer the opportunity and the products to more people at one time. Show the products and talk about the benefits of joining you and your company. Most distributors spend only 100 +/- hours each year during which they face their prospects with the expectation of closing the sale. This is based on 52 Home Parties, one a week at an average of 2 hours per Party. It might take you more or less time but that should be an average including driving time, the Party and any paperwork you might have. Notice how the 1952 hours have dwindled in number and how each of the 100 hours has mounted in value. (See Chart #2).

Using Your Time Better Brings You More Money

Time is so valuable and it slips through our fingers. Don't waste time. You get up in the morning with best intentions, and by nightfall, you are disappointed in what you did not get accomplished. You know you can do more than you did during the day. You know we wasted time. Valuable time. The next days turn into weeks, months and years. Finally, you are getting older and start regretting what could have been. Time is ticking.

Tick tock, tick tock.

THE PARTY PLAN GOAL
=Host ONE Party a week

How are you going to use your time?

Decide what action you are going to take, it's up to you.

Time = Money

How To Make The Maximum Amount Of Money In Party Plan

Hold enough Parties to show your product so that you can consistently sell and recruit monthly. Obviously, Parties are not going to yield their money's worth to you unless the Parties you hold produce a maximum amount of business. Master presenting, recruiting and selling skills to achieve maximum success.

The Party Plan Rule

It is never consistent with true salesmanship to accept an order which represents goods or services that the buyer cannot use, does not need, or for any other reason, known to the distributor, ought not to buy. Don't just "*get the sale.*" Instead get the customer to want to do business with you again.

Move Products Out Of The Warehouse

Companies have warehouses full of products and they pay distributors to move the product out of the warehouse and into the hands of the masses. Having Parties is just *one* way to do this. Your check reflects the value you bring to the corporation. The more products you move out of their warehouse, the larger your check.

The Home Party Concept

The Party idea is to increase the number of people you share your products and opportunity with so you can move more products. It's not hard. It's easy. It just takes focus, concentration and Host coaching. The concept is to increase the number of sales, recruits and prospects you get per Party. The more times you share the benefits of the products and opportunity, the more people will join you, and the bigger and faster your business grows.

Once you get the Party Plan rolling, it's like a train that has left the station. It's unstoppable.

Be grateful instead of hateful. Have an attitude of gratitude that you discovered PARTY PLAN

The Party Plan Wheel

There are 4 simple sections to this plan. It's not hard to do Party Plan once you see how easy it is.

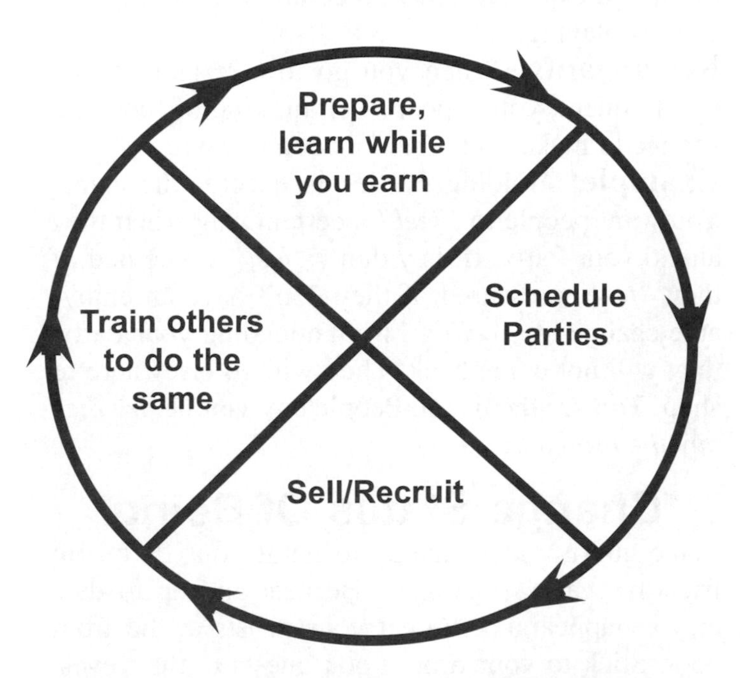

Persistency Counts When It Is Applied Properly

Persistence in scheduling Parties and perseverance in your efforts to sell your products and opportunity are essential to Party Plan success. Focus on the next Host who will realize that they will benefit from having *YOU* do a Party for them. Sell having a Party with YOU! Persistently pursue your goals.

Sometimes **"no"** is just a slow **"yes."**

Prepare for abundance!

Goals Are Dreams With Deadlines

Make today *THE* day that you say: *"No more, I will not live like I am living today, I will no longer settle for mediocrity. I have made a decision to decide to go for greatness. No one can make me do anything, I must desire to change my way of life for the better forever. I am willing and eager to start my climb to the top. It starts today!"*

Next: Take action: Schedule one Party a week. Get on with it. *Start now*. Start today!

Party Plan Is NOT Only About Building Relationships

Party Plan is NOT only about building relationships. It's about building a business. It's about selling the benefits to the Host about *what's in it for them* to hold a Party with you. It's about recruiting others to do the same. It's a business, it's not about building a huge group of friends. Friendships and relationships will come and go and some will grow very deep roots. The idea of Party Plan is to build a business through showing several people your product and opportunity at the same time. Focus on building a business that will bring you residual income.

NOT SUCCEEDING IS NOT AN OPTION

Word Of Mouth Marketing

You are a walking advertisement for your company. You are a walking billboard. If you move products, you will be valued by your company. Your success or failure are up to you in Party Plan. No one else controls what you do in life. People buy you first. You are the ticket.

You Are The Ticket

When you purchase a ticket to a sporting event, a movie, a train ride, a plane ride, or any other reason, what does that ticket *really mean*? It's just a piece of paper, right? It means that you have paid for something that is going to change your state of being. You hope your team wins, that the movie entertains you, that the train is on time and gets you where you wish to go, that plane takes you to a different climate. **You are like the ticket that someone buys when they schedule a Party with you. They hope it will be successful. They expect it to be. You are the ticket.**

You Are A State Changer

When people feel a certain way, they either return for that feeling or they don't return. It is up to the distributor to create a feeling so that guests want to return. It's not just about the product, it's the feeling people get when they are at your Party. The more of a *"good feeling"* they get, the more interested they will be in what you are saying.

Examples:

Church: In church, how do you expect to *feel*? Possibly, you expect to *feel* like you will be a better person. You have an expectation of the fact that how you *"feel"* is going to happen. If it does not happen, or you don't *"feel"* welcomed, normally you might *"feel"* like you are not attending the right church for you and, you begin to look for a change.

Travel: When you jet off to a destination that you have been to before you expect to *"feel"* a certain way when you arrive.

Sporting Events: When you go to a sporting event you expect to *"feel"* a certain way while your team is playing.

Restaurants: When you go to a restaurant that you frequent, you expect a certain kind of food and service to make you *"feel"* a certain way.

Example: Holding Parties is exactly the same. You want people to *"feel"* a certain way when they attend your Party. If they don't *"feel"* welcomed, if they *"feel"* pressured, if they don't have an enjoyable change of *"feeling"* from attending your Party, they will not come back. They will go elsewhere to shop. **You** are the ticket. People buy **you** *before they buy the product.*

Change States Of Being

Make guests *"feel"* happy to be at your Party. Be friendly, warm, organized. Be neat and up to date in your appearance. Greet your guests at the front door. Stick to your time. Look guests in their eyes. Be sincerely interested in helping guests select the right products. Enjoy the Party yourself.

Remember: Interested is interesting. Take a sincere interest in your guests and they will *"feel"* like you care and will trust you. If they trust you, they will like you, if they like you, they will buy from you, schedule Parties with you or join you.

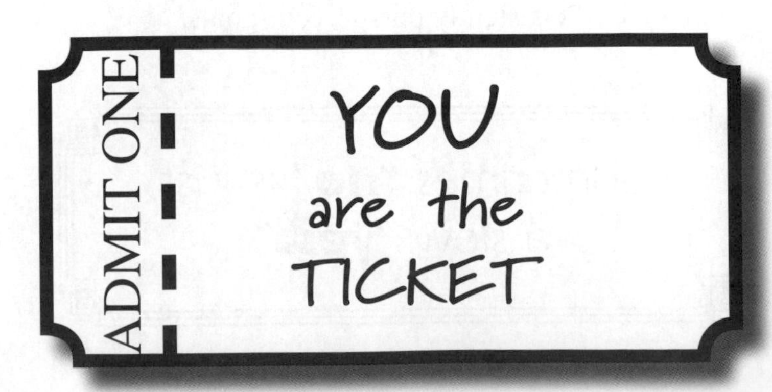

Plan To Go To The Top Of Your Pay Plan

Discover what you are doing that is profitable and what is NOT profitable as well. You are on your way to the top when your goal is having at least 4 Parties a month. One a week. When you schedule Parties, the next step is to get others to do the same. You want thousands of distributors doing Parties. If you don't recruit in your area, because you are worried you will lose business, think about this: someone else might come into your area and start recruiting. Wouldn't you rather those distributors be in your successline? Using The Booking Letter (see page 61), prospecting, overcoming objections, leading prospects to joining and teaching them to do the same is the only way to the top in Party Plan. Concentrate, focus, and plan to go to the top of your compensation plan.

Make a plan
Plan to work
Work your plan.

Plan Ahead
It was not raining
when Noah
built the ark!

Plan The Next Day's Work

Do not consider your workday finished until you have outlined a detailed work schedule for the next day. When you have a planned order of work, your scheduled Parties will become more efficient and effective and you will have made it possible to earn the full value of your selling time.

The first 2 weeks of the month concentrate on selling, the last 2 weeks of the month concentrate on recruiting, scheduling more Parties and training others to do the same.

An Easy Way To Plan

1. **Start today.**
2. **Contact your friends and everyone you know and next...**
3. **Tell the world what you plan to do and do it.**
4. **Take urgent action.**
5. **Stay fired up for as long as it takes.**

Two little words that make a gigantic difference:

> ***"I will persist until I succeed!"***
> **- Og Mandino**

Present Like a Pro

We are in the business of selling. Selling includes informing, persuading, inspiring and entertaining. Remember, the opposite of setup is upset. The more you control the former, the less you will become the latter. No matter how you slice it, your guests really want only one question answered:

"What's in it for me?"

Questions Guests At Parties Ask Themselves

1. Will I hear anything that will help me save or make money?
2. Will I hear anything that will save time?
3. Will I hear anything that will reduce stress, anxiety or confusion?
4. Who are you?
5. What are you going to talk about?
6. When will you be through?
7. What's in it for me?

The WidthVersus Depth Principle

The goal is to have at least 5 direct distributors building their businesses in your successline. We call these top direct 5 distributors *"legs"*.

Build wide for income, deep for security.

Solid width, stable income.

limited width, mediocre income.

EVERY EAGLE KNOWS A SPARROW AND EVERY SPARROW KNOWS AN EAGLE

Ask everyone to have a Party with you!

Practice The 3 Foot Rule

Speak to everyone who comes within 3 feet of you. Always have your business cards with you. Activity breeds productivity. Your mouth is the best advertising tool you have. Use it!

"It's my life,
it's now or never."
-Crush

Act As If

Step up your personal goals and you will give yourself and your business a dramatic push up the ladder of success. Don't settle for being just an *average* producer when, with a little extra effort, you can become a *top* producer, **one of the best**.

How to do better: Set an income goal that has definite, periodic increases. As soon as you set a higher income goal, you will begin to think of yourself as a bigger earner. *Thinking* like a top distributor is half the battle. It makes you want to *act* like one. Act *"as if"* you have achieved your goals!

Result: You will become more confident every day. Repeat this to yourself several times a day: "*Every day in every way I am getting better and better at this*."

Important: The mere fact of setting goals won't do the trick. It's only a start. The important thing to do is to "*energize*" your goals, put some action into your hopes, dreams, thinking and above all, hard work. *You can't stroll to a goal!*

"Fake it Till You Make It"... Worked for Me!

Have Faith And Total Belief That You Will Succeed In Holding Parties

YOU *MUST* BELIEVE:

1. THAT YOU WILL SUCCEED.
2. THAT YOU WILL PERSIST.
3. THAT YOU WILL GET TO THE TOP.
4. THAT YOU WILL RE-EVALUATE YOURSELF MONTHLY AND MAKE CHANGES IF YOUR ARE NOT MAKING PROGRESS.
5. THAT PROGRESS BEGINS ONE STEP AT A TIME. THERE IS NO SUDDEN LEAP TO GREATNESS.
6. SUCCESS IS WORKING DAY BY DAY.

3 Beliefs For Lasting Success

1. **It must change now.**
2. **I must change it now.**
3. **I can change it now.**

"Failure is not an option"
-Jayne Leach, FLP,UK

Parties Are Fun

Buyers favor the distributor from whom they can get the most benefit. Gone is the day of the salesman who went around handing out expensive cigars, slapping people on the back, and entertaining lavishly. Some distributors still act as if buyers want to buy from the distributor filled with hype rather than from the distributor who presents the most beneficial opportunity. Benefits are now preferred to cigars. Keep your Parties fun, fast paced and lively. Remember, to sell the benefits to the guests.

Network Marketing is not a giant adult daycare for losers. Today it is a viable, respectable business. It is considered a serious profession.

Make Party Plan your profession

ONE HOME PARTY A WEEK BRINGS FREEDOM MY WAY

Before You Start Your Drive To The Top

Before you start your drive to becoming a top distributor, make sure you are willing to go all the way. If you answer *"no"* to any of the following questions, you may *prefer* to be average. To start to the top, you have to prepare to change.

1: Am I willing to sacrifice some pleasures and comforts to reach my goal?

2: Is my attitude right, do I enjoy my work?

3: Am I completely *"sold"* on my products?

4: Am I constantly learning to make my efforts more effective?

5: Do I bend over backwards to give my customers the service they deserve?

6: Do I really understand my customers, associates and friends?

7: Am I willing to invest in feeding my mind by buying books, tapes, attending seminars and conventions?

The Goal Is To Sell Products AND Sell The Opportunity

Party Plan is like an airplane. To make it take off *you must sell products and recruit others to do the same*. Think of selling as one wing of the airplane and recruiting as the other. The tail is the training of how to do both. Concentrate on selling and recruiting rather than on building purely personal relationships. Master Party Plan to build a strong, lasting business. At every Party, you MUST sell products and sell the opportunity of doing the same. Sell yourself, you are the ticket.

Here is how: Gear your thinking and activities more in terms of *actual orders* than in terms of friendly chats.

Note To Single Parents

I was a single mother for 5 years. I never complained. I didn't have time to have a pity Party for myself. It was really rough, but the children and I survived. I didn't skip a beat. I was going to be successful. I was not going to be denied the lifestyle. I had no idea if I would ever marry again so I didn't want to waste one second waiting around for someone to financially take care of me. I never wanted to ask a man for money again. I never wanted to justify what I was spending again. I never wanted to buy a man a gift with an "*allowance*" he gave me. I never wanted to consider or consult a man ever again for anything I wished to spend money on the rest of my life. If you are a single parent, you will work your business differently than those with partners. It's just the way it is. Don't find yourself feeling sorry for yourself; get on with building your business. The benefit to being a single parent is that you don't have a negative partner to consider or to hold you back. Don't complain, press onward for yourself and for your children's sake. Do not be denied. Don't let having children be an excuse. Make them your reason why you will succeed.

I put out flyers all over town. We went to 4 parks a day, the zoo, the airport, shopping malls, dance studios, elementary schools, and everywhere *with my children* to pass out flyers... for 5 years.

Your Very Own "*Round To It*"

To It

Do you ever hear yourself or others say that you will start building a business or schedule more Parties when ***you get around to it***? The top distributors don't wait around making excuses. Right now, some place in the world, someone is quitting Network Marketing while someone else is joining, while someone else is doubting that they can succeed and yet others are charting their way to the top. Life does not wait on you. Life is ticking by right now. What you do today will manifest itself in 10-20 years. It's called choices. We choose our own path every day. What's hard to do, is also easy to do. It's simply up to the individual to make a decision to take personal responsibility for their own life. If you start today, build a Party Plan business and stick around, you will have an amazing lifestyle. *What you work toward every day and you ardently desire, must ultimately come to pass*...I said that to myself at least a bizillion times.

A Sense Of Urgency

The president of a successful company was asked what it took to get *to the top*. "*The same thing it took to get started,*" he replied. "*A sense of urgency about getting things done.*" No matter how intelligent or able you may be, if you don't have a sense of urgency, now is the time to start to develop it. The world is full of competent people who honestly intend to do things tomorrow, or as soon as they get *around to it.* Their accomplishments, however seldom match those of less talent who are blessed with a sense of the importance of getting started now.

A Modern Attitude Is Needed For Achieving Success

The Host who already finds it beneficial to give you a substantial amount of business will listen with receptive ears to facts that show how they can profitably use your products. Do not ask someone to schedule a Party as a sort of favor to you, without bothering to show the Host ***how THEY*** can benefit from having a Party with you. Keep the attitude of *what is in it for others*.

The Natural Born Distributor Is A Myth

Any normal person, who is interested can learn and can succeed at Party Plan. There is no such thing as a *"natural born sales person or distributor"*. Every top distributor is a student of Network Marketing. They refuse to give in or give up. They press on. There is much to learn from the top distributor in your successline.

Build An Idea Bank

The more ideas you can learn, the more sales and recruits you will get. Once you become idea hungry, you will get ideas all the time. To preserve the ideas that come to you at odd moments, keep a journal near by. Jot down the ideas you read, or hear, or see. Go to seminars taught by people who will share their ideas that get results. Then put them into action. Always be listening for new ideas.

Brain Flashes

From time to time as you get fired up about doing Parties, you will get ideas that pop into your mind. Don't let them escape. Write them down, call your own cell phone and leave yourself a message. Email yourself. Don't lose those precious thoughts.

Work On Self-Confidence

Being confident is important in Party Plan. The Host and guests invariably look for self-confidence in the distributor who presents to them. They want to do business with a distributor who knows what they are selling. Many consider the distributor's self-confidence way before agreeing to having a Party. The more you learn, the more you earn, and the more self-confident you become.

Have Absolute Confidence

Distributors with *absolute confidence* in the superiority of the benefits of their product and opportunity should have no challenge with presenting. In fact, they enjoy presenting to find out what selling and recruiting techniques they use get results. Totally believe in what you are selling, your belief will come shining through. You must believe in what you are selling.

The Mind Control Box

As you realize how powerful Parties can be, you will begin to believe more in yourself. You will begin to condition your mind by storing your subconscious mind that which mysteriously directs many of your actions and ambitions. Its called the:

"*Mind Control Box.*"

Control your thoughts to control your actions.

Say to yourself: *"As I learn more about Party Plan, the ideas will soon become part of my daily activity, the ideas will also seep into my other mind, that part of my mind which never sleeps, which creates my dreams. I will not be denied a fabulous future. I will make my fortune in Party Plan. I will search the world for ideas and take urgent action. My new life starts today."*

Here Is An Easy Way To Get Started

1: **Believe in your ability to reach your goals:** Just as right thinking will energize your enthusiasm, so will belief in your personal power to reach the earning goals you have set for yourself. Belief helps to generate enthusiasm. Without enthusiasm, and a powerful belief that you WILL succeed, you will get nowhere. You must believe in the Party Plan to make it work for you. When you believe it will work, you will be able to schedule more Parties than those with small beliefs. Massive belief brings massive confidence.

2: **Copy a distributor who is getting results:** Take an objective look at the person you *know* is a top distributor. Not those who quit the business to train others how to do the business. Not those who jump from company to company. Not those who are trying to do several programs at once. Notice that wherever the top distributors go, they carry an air of self-confidence. Nothing about the top distributor hints defeat. Press onward and upward towards your goal. **Here is how:** Expect to win, to succeed, to achieve. Because you expect to win, believe you will succeed...and here is what shows up... your attitude becomes inspiring to others. Now... take a...

3: **Look at yourself:** How do you shape up? Do you *look* like a top distributor? Would others say you have that *air of self-confidence?* Well... if you don't, you should.

I'll Do It!

Balance = How To Do It All

How did I schedule Parties, recruit others, train them to do the same, do the paperwork, pass out literature, be a team member, attend meetings, attend seminars, attend conventions, keep in touch with my Hosts, hold meetings, answer emails, exercise, read, feed my mind, be a good daughter/mother/friend and neighbor, enjoy my hobbies, go out with friends, be entertained, get rest AND stay fired up for years? How can this be a reality? If it's too good to be true, it's too good to be true. Is it necessary to balance everything? You might have to sacrifice doing some things you are doing now to be able to do and have more later in life. The goal in life is to be balanced in all areas of life. Why do so many people talk about balance? If you truly want to succeed in Party Plan, you might have to be out of balance for a few years. But not forever. You might have to make some serious choices, and say goodbye to friends who are wasting your lifetime. You might have to get up earlier, stay up later. The reality is, being successful is a choice.

Put a sign on your office door that says:

If you have nothing to do, don't do it here!

The answer my friend is not blowing in the wind, the answer is truly right in your own hands.

****

It's about the choices you make in life.

When you set valid, achievable goals, the universe will rearrange itself to accommodate you.

Find a need and fill it, Find a hurt and heal it

Every Single Person Who Wants To Succeed Can

It's not the universe that holds people back, it's their choices. Think long and hard about how you want your life to look in 5-10-15-20-25 years from now. You can't wait around until...the time to get to work building your future is now.

All I want is everything!

Set your sights for higher earnings in Party Plan
* Smart choice! *

"What you ardently desire, and are willing to work towards every single day, must ultimately come to pass."

-Somerset Maugham

Smart Time Management

1. **Turn off the TV** until 11 p.m. or until you have Parties booked for 3 months in advance.
2. **Do not stay on the phone with** friends, family or distributors for more than 10 minutes until you have Parties booked for 3 months in advance. Don't waste time on the phone.
3. **Don't kid yourself** about what you are doing. *Your activity will either promote you or expose you. This is not a hobby. It's a business.*
4. **When you cook,** prepare double amounts and freeze an extra family serving in pie pans with foil on the top and put a sticker on the top with the date that you put it in the freezer. Pop one in the oven on Party nights.
5. **Use paper plates** on Party nights. Simplify.
6. **Have two Party outfits** of clothes always ready to go so you don't have to think of what to wear.
7. **Turn down invitations** to being the Scout Leader, the Sunday School teacher, the Room Mother, the mother/father who goes on all the field trips, etc. When the teachers asked me to bring cookies to Parties at school, I warmed up Oreo cookies, the children loved them and never knew that I didn't bake cookies. Choose to work your business when your children are young so that you will have more time with them later in life.
8. **Make an "*I am willing to work for*" list.** Be honest with yourself. Only put on that list that which you truly want. Work to get it.
9. **Do not use your children as an excuse** why you cannot do Parties, make your children your reason *why* you are doing Parties.
10. **Develop your opening** and closing scripts to use at the Party to get the biggest results.

Change your thinking from
"I can't afford to"
to
"I can't afford not to!"

Do not give in or quit when you are discouraged... instead...

Never ever give up.
It's always too soon to quit.
Focus.
Schedule more Parties.

The fortune is in the
Follow up

I like it, I love it!
I want some more of it!

Learn From Those Who Walk The Walk

Attend seminars led by distributors with proven track records, not those who have quit to become trainers. Many corporations try to control distributors to only go to seminars they encourage or recommend. If your business is not growing and your company is trying to control who you listen to, put some thought in to that. You are an INDEPENDENT contractor. Ask yourself, *what is the company worried about, why are they worried if I listen to someone who has a proven track record?* Be worried with management which tries to control where you get new ideas. *Search the world for new ideas.* Read the books the top distributors do, forget about reading the books the quitters read. Search for ideas.

Today's Top Distributors Are Serious Students Of Network Marketing

Today's distributor must have a capacity and interest for learning and must *want* to study Party Plan. The times **demand** that the distributor be eager to learn. Party Plan today relies fully as much on educating the prospect as it does on persuading them. Before a guest at a Party can be educated, the distributor must get educated.

> "Before financial growth can occur, personal growth must occur."
>
> **-Jim Rohn**

Stay Aware To New Ideas

We are living in a dynamic world in which monumental changes that affect us occur while we are not looking. You cannot be blamed for missing the new developments in all the fields of human activity; you don't have the time and may not have the interest to keep up with the discoveries of scientists and psychologists. But, if you miss the impact of the developments as they touch your own business as a distributor, you can lose orders. Stay current and continue to look for and use new ideas.

Idea: Have a healthy respect for your Upline's or mentors *constructive* suggestions for selling and recruiting of your product or opportunity. The involved modern Upline alerts their sales force to improved selling and recruiting techniques as they are developed. Top Upline's find out what is happening by attending conferences, by exchanging ideas with other leaders and studying those who are getting results. Determine the simplest and most direct methods of attaining the ultimate goal of increasing your sales. Pay close attention to new ideas. Try them.

Always be the student. Today's readers are tomorrow's leaders.

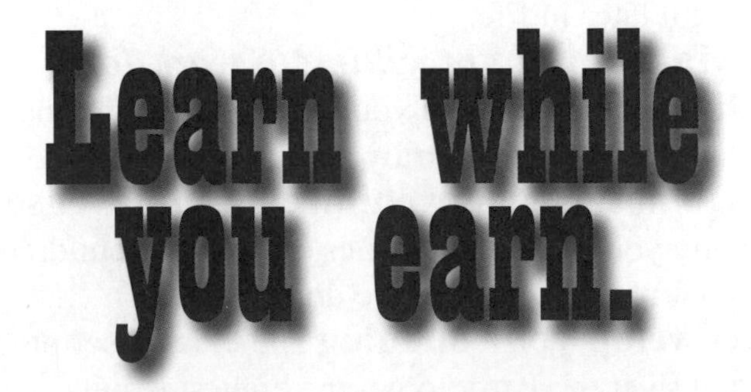

Go for a
paycheck
not a playcheck

Top Techniques That Work

1. **Answer emails** in a timely fashion.
2. **Attend meetings**, conference, conventions and training sessions.
3. **Be accessible** to help others understand Party Plan and help them get started on their path to the top.
4. **Use survey** interviews.
5. **Handle complaints** and adjustments calmly.
6. **Ignore the critics:** There are no statues built to remember them.
7. **Do not let one situation** nor one person have permission to upset one precious moment of your lifetime.
8. **Stay faithful** to your dreams.
9. **Use The Booking Letter:** Share this with your entire successline. (see page 61)
10. **Work hard in the first years** of your business; from 8 to faint.

There Are Only 2 Ways To Make Money

1. **Through individual effort or...**
2. **By motivating people**

Only one is limitless

Party Plan Includes Many Non-Selling Duties

When you decide you are going to the top of your plan, be aware that it is more than just selling, recruiting, and holding Parties. There are a lot of other parts of the business that build the foundation for an incredible residual income forever.

1. **Always look for opportunities** to remind the customer that you have *their* interests in mind.
2. **Attend conferences** and seminars to increase your knowledge.
3. **Keep records** and filing reports.
4. **Keep samples,** kit, literature and related items neat, fresh and up to date.
5. **Run contests** that boost sales and recruiting in your successline.
6. **Schedule phone calls.**
7. **Send customers** literature describing new products.
8. **Send thank you notes.**
9. **Stay in contact** with successline via telephone and email.
10. **Teleconferencing classes** example: *The Really Big Show*. Register at www.janruhe.com.
11. **Train distributors** to raise their selling and recruiting ability.
12. **Use The Booking Letter.** (see page 61)
13. **Watch deadlines** as though your business depends on reaching them. Because it does.

The 3 D's:

Desire. Dedication. Determination.

Increase Number Of Customers/Hosts/Recruits

Every Network Marketer who is aiming *for top achievement* must increase the number of new customers and distributors. To do this *you must* increase the number of prospects, the number of calls, and the number of Parties that could result in more sales and more recruits. Always be working with 20 new prospects. You will be busy building a massive business if you prospect and follow up. You will get the correct pace by how often you close. Always be closing too often and too soon so that you can learn how to quickly take a prospect to being a Host or recruits.

A prospect is only a suspect before they become a prospect.

Recognize The Value Of Those Who Care About Sharing Ideas With You

Today's top Uplines, and trainers, understand the demands on the distributor's time, and step up their training programs in order to speed up the development of *top notch* producers. The modern Upline aids distributors in their belief and ideas to schedule more Parties and to continue to strive for greatness in teaching others to do the same. If you happen to be in such a successline, recognize the value of their Party Plan training efforts. To find an Upline who truly cares about their distributors is not to be taken for granted. To find an Upline who is accessible and puts your needs first is rare. If you have an Upline like that, you are blessed. Put into action what you are taught. A great Upline, trainer or mentor is priceless.

Step Up To Good Life!

Want People To Value You As An Excellent Trainer?

In the 1990's, Network Marketing changed enormously. In the 90's some distributors tried the business, couldn't make it, quit and set themselves up as pros or as *"experts."* Others *"retired"* and set themselves up as *"expert"* trainers without ever getting to the top. Others were desperate to be speakers. If you want to be a credible, professional speaker in Network Marketing, you must get to the top of your Pay Plan. Then you are believable. Then you bring value. *Why listen to a quitter tell you how to do the business?* You don't need a university accreditation to be believable. Results speak loud and clear. People want to hear from those who are recruiting, selling and teaching others to do the same. No one wants to hear from those who do not work the business or who quit. Being a speaker up in front of the room trying to teach that which you have not done is really boring to distributors. Build a Network Marketing business through Party Plan, then others will value your training.

Get More Energetic

It is a privilege to be in the presence of someone who has positive energy and enthusiasm. *Let that person be you.* Every day we are given the gift of time, but we don't know what will be reserved to tomorrow. Energy can be drained and the biggest thief of energy is stress and worry. Make a special effort to schedule more Parties and to build your business daily. Reduce stress, make more money.

Today
I will
succeed.

I'll tell you why
.....
Because I have
FAITH, COURAGE
and
ENTHUSIASM!

A Private Memo To Myself About Me

To: (Your Name)
Date:

My present weekly income is
______________________________.

My job title, 45 weeks from now is
______________________________.

My weekly income, 45 weeks from now is __________________.

That's it. Sign it, and tuck it away. Don't talk to anyone about it except your partner or spouse. Do it now...NOW! I am not asking you for a long list of what you are willing to work for or what you wish to achieve. **Why?** Because it's not necessary for me to know those things. Those are for another list for you to make. If you change your income and your title as much as I think you have indicated on this private list to yourself, then all the material things you desire will begin to come your way. Record your *"I am willing to work for list"* in your Success Journal to keep you on course and refer to it often.

Be careful what you wish for, you just might get it!

Can My Area Get Saturated By People Holding Parties?

Try to saturate your area. In over 20 years, I don't know of an area saturated by Parties worldwide. ***Try*** to be the leader of the successline doing the saturating. One year we almost did it. We had Parties going on every day, sometimes 2 to 5 a day in my neighborhood. Everyone was getting invited to a Party almost daily. That lasted for only 2 months. Some distributors got worried and quit. I stuck around. The following year, many of *their* Hosts, called and scheduled Parties with me. Stick around. That flurry of business in that one area only lasted 2 months. Never quit trying to saturate your area.

There Is Always A Solution To A Challenge

The creative distributor has learned that there exists a solution to every challenge. If you are stuck and can't schedule a Party, re-examine what you are doing with your time. Work on your presentation skills. Right this minute, thousands of Parties are being held worldwide. The Party Plan is alive and well. It's not Party Plan that is the challenge. For things to change you must change. For things to get better, you must get better.

Important: A solution does exist when you hit a brick wall. If all doors seem locked, look for an open window. Don't give up. If you are constantly scheduling Parties, you won't have time to get discouraged.

Party Plan is not get rich quick scheme.
It calls for a LOT of hard work.

You Never Know Who Is In Your Audience

Be careful about stating your personal opinions at the Party. You never know who is in your audience. Here are some examples:

1: I once said in a Party, *"This is so easy to do, it's not rocket science!"* After my Party, a gentleman came up to me and said, *"I am a rocket scientist at NASA, so you don't think I could do this? I was so interested until you said that?"*

2: One time I said, *"This is just like xyz company only it's so much better!"* Afterwards a young mother said, *"My mother is the top distributor in that company, she put me through school being a distributor for them. I don't think I would join your company with someone like you."* I learned a very valuable lesson to never criticize another company EVER.

3: I was in a small house giving a Party presentation and the sales were very low. I was really nice to the Host and the next day she called and said her sister would like to Host a Party for me. I followed up right away and her sister had a $2,000+ Party, served champagne and caviar, had a mansion packed with friends who were *eager* to buy *and* I met my ultimately best life long friend, Libby.

WHEN YOU GET TO THE TOP...
LIFE WILL NEVER BE THE SAME

Remember Names

Top distributors are fully aware of the value of remembering their Host names. Use the Host's name without overdoing it. This is important in the beginning of the Party when repeating the Host's name will make everyone there realize you are recognizing the Host and some will be thinking *"I would like to be recognized like this."* Every time you use the name of your Host, look at them.

Why? By looking directly at your Host you will appear more sincere and close contact can be reached more readily. Make sure you pronounce your Host's name correctly.

Why? The more difficult the name, the more important it is that you are saying it correctly. Do NOT mispronounce the Host's name.

Get People To Remember YOUR Name

Most people can remember the name of your company instead of yours. Then when they are approached 5 or 6 times about the opportunity, they can't remember you or the first or second or third person who actually told them about the business opportunity or asked them to Host a Party. So, it's so important for guests to all remember ***your*** name.

> *"We are living in a material world and I am a material girl!"*
>
> **-Madonna**

Use Your Business Cards As Name Tags

Take some business cards, a box of straight pins and a black marker to the Party. As people arrive, ask them to take your business card and have them write their first name with the marker on the card. Then PIN your business card on their shirt or blouse. They will go home with YOUR phone number or email address pinned on them. Clever!

Mention Your Name 6 Times

During your opening, the middle of your presentation, and your closing, mention your name at least **6** times. Make sure that your contact information is on every piece of literature you hand out or send.

Use Huge Stickers On Catalogs And Products

Put a HUGE sticker on the front of catalogs, on the front of your recruiting brochures with YOUR CONTACT INFORMATION on the FRONT. **Sell YOU**! Put your contact information on every product. Do everything you can to have people remember **your name** and let them know that if they would like to schedule a Party, to schedule it with **YOU**!

Here is why: Many customers do not know how Network Marketing works. They just think, have a Party, get FREE stuff. Period. Their thinking is not: "*I need to have a Party with this distributor because they are the one who gave me the idea in the first place and they will get a commission.*"

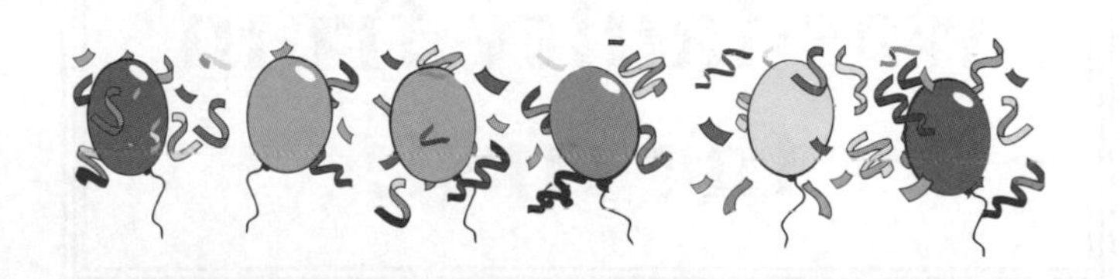

Tell me what you want

Put Your Contact Information On Everything

Avoid: Forgetting to put your contact information on your literature. Many guests keep literature in stacks to look at a later date. When they get to your literature and your name is difficult to find, they will either look up your company online, in the phone book or will start asking their friends if they know of a distributor. Without you knowing it, your literature travels. People take stacks of brochures to friends or relatives homes and you never know where an order can come from.

All Literature Must Be In Perfect Shape

Put all messy literature in the trash. Do not send out literature with coffee stains or rips or portions missing and especially don't send out the hundredth photo copy that no one can read. Everything that leaves your office should be perfect.

Faith that fizzles before the finish was faulty from the first.

Change Your Attitude If You Are Making These Mistakes

1: You feel that you are already getting a substantial volume of business from someone and it is nice to *"leave well enough alone."*

2: You think: *"Well, my friends know me so well that if they were interested in having a Party they would call me."*

3: You assume that the Host has reasons for not joining your opportunity. *The burden of stating the reasons and benefits of why someone should join rests upon the distributor, and not on the buyer.*

4: When someone decides to buy your products or join your opportunity, you don't have the courage to suggest a larger order. The only risk you run in suggesting a higher limit is that the customer will not follow your suggestion. But, most of the time they will, if the distributor shows it is profitable to them. Always ask, *"How many do you want?"*

Prosperity and abundance are coming my way.

Carpé Diem, seize the day!

Read Powerful Daily Quotes

There are many places to find inspiring quotes. There are books filled with quotes. They are available online, in magazines, newspapers, and everywhere. At your meetings, swap quotes that have motivated you and empower each other.

"You can have everything you want, if you go after it. But you will have to want it. The desire for success must be so strong within you that it is the very breath of your life, your first thought when you awaken in the morning, your last thought when you go to bed at night."

- Charles Popplestone

"The longer I live, the more I am certain that the great difference between men, between the feeble and the powerful, between the great and the insignificant, is the energy, invincible determination, a purpose, once fixed, and then death or victory."

- Sir Thomas Buxton

"I have always believed that anybody with a little guts and the desire to apply himself can make it, can make anything he wants to make of himself."

-Willie Shoemaker

If You Continue To Do What You Have Always Done, You Will Continue To Get What You Have Always Gotten

The Party Plan Creed

I feed my mind positive thoughts.
My fabulous future starts today.
I master my dreams.
I am the captain of my ship.
I have a burning desire to succeed.
I have the Rhino Spirit.
I will achieve. I help others along the way.
I am a self-starter.
I am proactive not reactive.
I do more than is expected.
I come from contribution.
I focus on what is in this for the Host.
I motivate myself and will stay fired up, forever. I will not be denied the lifestyle.
I am going to the top...

Watch *my* smoke!

STP

See The People

Sell The Product

Seek Total Prosperity

Sponsor The Persistent

Share The Plan

Sell The Plan

Success Takes Persistence

Come From An Abundance Consciousness-Self Talk

In the past, I accepted failure and the pain it brought me. No more. I now reject it and am prepared for wisdom and ideas which will guide me out of the dark part of my past into the sunlight of wealth, position and happiness far beyond my wildest dreams. I now will have extravagant dreams. I must take action right away because I do not have the luxury of eternity. I must practice the art of patience because success never comes in haste. I will no longer live the life of an onion, as the onion plant is old in 9 weeks. I will now live like the king of trees, the olive tree that lives for 100 years. And how will this all be accomplished? For I have not succeeded yet and am just gathering new information. I do not have the experience of achieving greatness and I refuse to live in self pity any more. The answer is so simple. I will begin my journey to the top unencumbered with the weight of unnecessary knowledge. I will not get analysis paralysis, I choose to begin. I am running out of lifetime and must succeed. I will learn while I earn. Nature has already blessed me with instinct that I must use. Experience is the best teacher and I need to start getting more and more experience. I am going for greatness and realize that what I have learned so far in life is to prevent more failure rather than to gain success, for what is success but a state of mind. Among 1,000 wise people, see if you can find 2 who define success in the same way. Failure is the inability to reach your goals in life, whatever they may be. Today I make a solemn oath that nothing will retard my new path. Nothing is going to block me from going to the top. I am sick and tired of being sick and tired. I am ready to throw off the chains of mediocrity and rise to the level of the eagle. I will not be tossed about like I am at sea without a ship. I will not be denied a fabulous future. I will not lose a day learning, from now on. It is a small price to pay for the happiness, success and abundance coming my way. I have swallowed the capsule of success. I will walk tall among others and they will know me, for today I am a new person with a new life. Why not me? Why not now? Today I start my new life. Today I shed my old self which has too long lived with disappointments and settled for a mediocre life. Today I am embarking on my new path in life. The career I have chosen is filled with opportunity yet many have failed and quit. I will not fail as the others, for in my hands I now hold the information which will guide me through the tough times. I will begin to dream again and go for greatness. Failure will no longer be my daily payment. I will think abundance and prosperity from today on.

-adapted from *Og Mandino*

"It's not a job, it's a way of life."

-The Lady of the Rings

Learn to think and say often. . ..

watch my smoke!

Work On Self-Improvement

Here is a quick test to take to honestly rate yourself. You can only cheat yourself by a biased rating. Cheating will seriously impair your changes for self-improvement. Rate yourself 4 on any question where you sincerely believe you are above average; 3 for good or average; 2 for fair or mediocre; and 1 for poor or weak. A total score of 70-80 means that you are above most distributors. This is undoubtedly reflected in your present, not past performance.

If your score is 55-70, it shows that you are an average distributor and can easily, with training readily improve yourself by getting training where you are weak. A score of 40-55 indicates that self-improvement should be started at once and diligently continued for as long as it takes for you to improve your skills. A score below 40 signifies that you are in real danger of failure and should adopt drastic, concentrated action to immediately take action to improve your skills. Don't kid yourself. The bottom line will tell your story. There are only 21 questions:

My fabulous future starts today!

	YES	NO
• Do I really want to succeed in Party Plan?	___	___
• Am I determined to succeed?	___	___
• Do I have the will to succeed?	___	___
• Am I willing to put forth concentrated effort and work hard?	___	___
• Am I willing to sacrifice some pleasures and comforts if need be?	___	___
• When adverse conditions arise, do I press on to reach my goals?	___	___
• Do I have a clear vision of my ultimate objective?	___	___
• Am I setting small goals as stepping stones to more easily attain my goal?	___	___
• Am I constantly learning to make my efforts more effective?	___	___
• Is my attitude right, so that I enjoy my business?	___	___
• Have I the right feeling for the company for which I represent?	___	___
• Am I completely sold myself on the products I sell.	___	___
• Do I have faith in my company to deliver product?	___	___
• Am I considerate of my distributors?	___	___
• Am I aware of all the motives that should impel me toward succeeding?	___	___
• Am I driven to go to the top?	___	___
• Do I care about my Host?	___	___
• Do I try to promote the Host feelings to gain good will?	___	___
• Do I command the confidence and respect of my guests?	___	___
• Do I look for the guests point of view and look for ways to meet the guests needs?	___	___
• Do I work to give the best customer service?	___	___
Total	___	___

Press on... have The Rhino Spirit

Give your knowledge boldly of your products and opportunity over and over...

Here is what you will get...

You will increase your sales, recruiting results and you will schedule more Parties!

Give your family everything you ever dreamed of

Predicting Personal Success

You can predict personal success by scheduling 52 Parties a year. One a week. When you see an average of 10 new guests at each Party, that's over 500 people in a year. It's an easy way to see many people and to tell about your opportunity and your products again and again. You will become well known for what you do. Prepare, study, keep trying new ideas, keep scheduling more and more Parties. The more people you present to the more opportunities you will have to move product and bring in others to do the same. You can only have outrageous results if you concentrate, focus and work persistently to schedule more Parties. You cannot get to the top by starting and stopping. Why not commit the next 3 to 5 years to building your fabulous future?

Positive Programming

It's been proven that people with positive attitudes achieve more in life. Those attitudes originate in our subconscious mind. A poor self-image, a *"can't-do-attitude,"* an idea that *"a lot of money is bad"* beliefs, buried deep in our subconscious, keep us from living up to our potential. When you begin to recruit you will help people and their programming. Reach out to your Upline or someone in your successline to teach you how to ask more people to join you. It's simply a numbers game. Tell yourself you CAN master Party Plan. After all, *you are simply the best.*

Self Talk: *Every day I am getting better and better at prospecting, recruiting and scheduling Parties.*

The Climb To The Top

As I reflect on how much I endured during the climb to the top, as well as the effort it took to reach that high goal, I can understand why most people are content to float through life, taking whatever comes easy. I found over time that there are three categories of distributors. That's it.

1. The non-achievers-passive distributors who wait around for something to happen. They are satisfied to be happy, content or even stagnate. They let others set goals for them and like to be told what to do. They like the security of stable conditions, they never leave the crowd because they are content to have shallow goals set for them and to do no more than what's expected, if that. They cheerfully participate on the team because that makes them feel that they are contributing in some way. But they won't take action on changing their lives.

2. The achievers-distributors who want to make things happen. They set their own goals that require a great deal of effort and persistence to reach, are self-motivated, self-directed, and self-determined. They don't depend on the government, they cherish their independence, are usually respected and well liked and tend to be activists who get involved. They work towards becoming successful, define success in material terms through status symbols and are desperate for recognition and significance. They are willing to put aside the fun-for-the-moment attitude in order to build better lives for themselves and will do without so that they can save money for security. **Their motto is:** *What the mind can conceive and believe, it can achieve.*

Where do you fit in?
Where do you really want to fit in?
Is it time to change groups?

3. The top achievers-top distributors. They will not settle for not being at the top, push themselves beyond normal human endurance, set goals that are considered unreachable by most people, constantly stretch to surpass their limitations and won't always be successful. In fact, they might fail because their reach may exceed their grasp. But often enough, they will reach their incredible goals, goals so high they'll shock even the achievers. They want their life to be epic, to take charge of their fate and destiny. Don't expect everybody to like or understand top achievers. The average person simply cannot grasp what it is that drives the top achiever to perform at such exhausting levels. They are driving forces beyond themselves, have caught a glimpse of the best life and will not settle for anything less, are constantly pushing against their own limits, deeply and personally involved in whatever they are doing, sometimes practically torturing themselves to achieve their high goals. *What is it that we admire most in these amazing achievers?* Do we admire them because they are different? *No, we admire them because they set high goals and work constantly at going for greatness! They are intent on succeeding. They are unstoppable. They are the top distributors.*

Next: I have no intention on telling you where you fit in, only you can make that decision. If you are still reading...I *suspect* you are an achiever on your way to being a top distributor. Most of the non-achievers will never get this far and if they do they hate it when they realize they are non-achievers and don't want to admit it. If you are an achiever and have a strong desire to become a top distributor, you can achieve big time An amazing future awaits you. Come to the table of plenty, there is a place set just for you. It's your turn to shine!

Touch your business every day in everyway

Set Yourself Up As *"The Expert"* Then Be One

For years people told me this did not work, but it did. **Say these words** and soon you will begin to believe them, then internalize them and they will come true: *"I am THE BEST presenter of (your products) in this town, village, city, etc. I love what I am doing.* ***You get the people to your Party, I will do the rest.*** *You can count on me to give a fun, fast-pace and exciting presentation that everyone will enjoy."* **Do this now: Declare this to yourself right now:**

"I am the expert in Party Plan in my company!"

Why not you be the best presenter in your area or company or country? Visualize everyone at the Party wanting to buy from you or join your successline! Once you start working on your skills daily and concentrate on learning every thing you possibly can about selling, recruiting, leadership and teaching others to do the same, you will become an expert soon.

5 Major Concerns You May Encounter

A guest's concern about your products or your opportunity should not be viewed as something negative to be brushed off as quickly as possible. Instead, a concern is something you need to address before continuing onward. There are 5 major concerns that you are likely to encounter:

1. No need.
2. No trust.
3. No interest.
4. No hurry.
5. No ability to decide or pay.

A distributor must correctly identify which concern is present. Responding to the wrong concern, no matter how brilliantly, will not bring you closer to scheduling a Party or making a sale.

Make everyone feel as though they have a flashing light on their forehead that says:

"Make me feel special."

-Mary Kay Ash

The Golden Rule

Do unto others as if they were you,
And you were receiver of that which they do;
Be free with your service for life is a school
Wherein you should live by the Golden Rule.
Be honest, be faithful, be truthful and kind.
Have pity for others, their needs bear in mind.
Have mercy, be thoughtful, forget ridicule.
For this is the goal of the Golden Rule.

Resist...Assist...Persist

If your intention is to genuinely be of service, and come from contribution, and get to the top of your Pay Plan, you must learn to resist, assist, and persist.

Resist...the temptation to back off too early when asked a question that might seem negative to you but actually is a concern of the guest. Listen carefully for the concern. If people are not interested in what you have to offer, then ask for a referral. Don't get your feelings hurt or feel rejected. Press on!

Assist...the guest in getting all of their questions answered and making the right choice for them.

Persist...without the intention of manipulating. Come from contribution. How can your product or opportunity help them?

Charisma

Charisma is something that cannot be taught. It is a fire of desire in your eyes, in your voice, the way you walk, the way you look, the way you carry yourself and the way that you put energy out into the world. This is not something you turn off and on. It is inside of you. Charisma attracts people. It is who you are when you are alone. It's what is deep inside of you. It's what gives you hope and courage and faith to keep on keepin' on. It's the deep desire and focus on the fact that you won't give in or give up. It's a happiness that you create for yourself. If you are angry, upset, mean, a jerk, nasty, unkind, critical, egotistical, wanting everyone to follow only you, that your way is the only way, you will never get to the top in Party Plan. You must change those parts of your personality and work on being more charismatic. Charismatic leaders have charismatic followers. They attract happy people. Can you teach yourself charisma? Yes, but only if you become a student of charisma. **Here is how:** Study charisma. Study it like it is under a microscope. Copy what charismatic distributors do.

Play Full Out

If you are not going after building your Party Plan business fully committed, you have no chance to get to the top. Decide upon your outcome, your final destination and play full out. Don't sit on the bench. The way to get your desires is to commit to get them.

GREAT PITCHERS NEED GREAT CATCHERS

Qualities Top Distributors Party Plan Share

The evidence is clear that most people can be top distributors if they are willing to study, concentrate and focus on their performance. Here are the characteristics of the highly successful distributors:

1. **Do not take *"no"* personally** and allow them to feel like a failure or rejected. They have high enough levels of confidence and self-esteem so that, although they might be disappointed, they are don't grieve or stew about the negative response.
2. **Take 100% acceptance of responsibility for results.** They do not blame the economy, the Pay Plan, the home office, their Upline, their parents, the weather, their spouse, other distributors or any one else. Instead, the worse things are, the harder they work to make negatives work to their advantage.
3. **Have above average ambition and total massive desire to succeed.** This is so key because it will affect your priorities and how you spend your time and with whom you associate.
4. **Have high levels of empathy.** They have the ability to listen to the guests and the Hosts. They come from how they can contribute to getting them what they want from their products or opportunity.
5. **Have ability to approach strangers** even when it's uncomfortable or they don't feel like it.
6. **Have above average will power** and total determination. No matter how tempted they are to give up, they persist toward goals.
7. **Are self-disciplined and self starters,** they don't need anyone to motivate them. They are motivated from within.
8. **Are impeccably honest with the Host and guests.** No matter what the temptation to lie, they resist and gain ongoing trust of their Hosts and guests.
9. **Are intensely goal-oriented.** They know what they are going after and how much progress they are making. They don't let distractions side track them. They learn to say *"Oh well"* and press onward.
10. **Have an attitude of gratitude.** They don't tear people down, they build people up. They look for the good in people.

Establishing Credibility

Credibility is largely a function of the distributors ultimate reason for succeeding or giving up. It is the distributor who sells the promise of value to begin with and who commits their company to supplying it. So, it is understandable that the Host and guests look to the distributor when value is not supplied.

1. **Know your product and opportunity.** Knowledge, or lack of it, is a critical factor in the Hosts appraisal of your presentation. If you know what you are doing, you will get referrals galore.
2. **Know what the Host and guests want.** The more you understand what people want, the more credible you will become as a seller of value.
3. **Give attention to detail.** When distributors cost people extra time or money, or distract them from buying, credibility as value-sellers suffers.
4. **Provide meaningful information.** When you do, you give credible information and the guests and Host will look to you for recommendations and advice.
5. **Follow through after the Party.** Take care to make sure that the products sold were delivered.

You Can't Afford To Follow The Crowd

Now is the time to take a stand to be unique, to be different. You can't afford to follow the crowd! Don't hold hands with someone not fired up and walk into the quicksand together or into the ocean to drown in misery together. The price tag is too much, the price is your life! Search for knowledge, strategies, systems, time management, spend more effort and know what the expenses will be. Be willing to do whatever it takes to reach your goals. This takes massive commitment...a no alternative, *"burn all bridges behind you leaving yourself no possible retreat"* commitment. The rest will be history and you will get there. The universe will rearrange itself to accommodate that which you truly want.

The C.R.S.I. Method

In conversations when you are standing in a line, or in a group or talking to prospects here is a method that opens the door...

Compliment: Say something nice to start the conversation.

Relate: Attempt to relate something that you have in common.

Share: Say: Have you ever heard of Network Marketing?

Invite: Invite them to a Party or to Host a Party.

> *Be rigorous about building your business*

Your Image

Why is it that some people can be successful in Party Plan and others fail? You can have all the right words to say, you can talk to a zillion people, you can have massive desire, you can use all the tools available, you can have a fired up attitude, you can have the most amazing smile, you can be the nicest person on earth, you can be at every seminar on the front row, you can learn what to say to overcome objections, you can be a team player and still not get anywhere. Many distributors don't realize what they do to cause distractions that they bring on themselves. Make sure you work on your image. Sweat the small stuff. Remember, you are the ticket.

You only get one chance to make a first impression. You never have a second chance. Your appearance is very important. When you are prospecting, training or presenting your products and opportunity, you don't want to distract people from listening to you. From now on, when you depart your home, you must look like you are succeeding. Don't pop into the supermarket to get one thing and run into a future Host and you look sloppy. They will cancel the Party and you won't know why. Your appearance in Party Plan is very important.

If you look exhausted or worn out, get some rest. If you come across as too busy, no one will want to Host a Party for you. People will get your rushed feeling and will give you every reason why they don't want to have a Party. Never talk about how "*busy*" you are. Isn't it interesting that people who tell you how "*busy*" they are have the time to tell you how "*busy*" they are? When you hear they are having a Party with someone else, you will have to stop and think WHY? Perhaps it's how you came across when talking with them or your appearance.

Teeth: Make sure you have clean teeth. If you have teeth missing, or teeth that are chipped, get them fixed. If you have capped front teeth, make sure that you have attractive caps. When you smile and you have teeth missing or chipped, although you have everything it takes to make it in Party Plan, your teeth will put people off.

Shoes: Don't wear scuffed shoes. Don't wear tennis shoes to a Party.

Voice: Pace your talking. If you have a thick accent or a quiet, soft, high-pitched voice, tape yourself and really listen to your voice. You can know everything there is to know but your voice might turn someone away from hosting a Party with you.

Laugh: Watch your laugh. If you have a hysterical laugh, loud, obnoxious laugh, people will not want to Host a Party for you.

Fingernails: Get a manicure regularly. You will be using your hands a lot in Party Plan. When you are presenting or demonstrating products, you want nice nails. Quit biting your nails. Its a big turn off to guests to see short, bitten off nails.

Hair: Have an up to date hair cut. Make sure your hair is clean. Don't go to a Party with messy, dirty, disheveled hair. You don't want people looking at your hair and not listening to you.

Glasses: Have up to date glasses. Keep current. Glasses change every year.

Clothes: No suits and ties. This is not the corporate world. Slacks and a nice shirt are perfect. Ladies, slacks, a dress, skirt and blouse is perfect. Look put together. Take the time to make yourself look the best you can.

Tattoos: Tattoos are very popular in some parts of our culture. But to people who do not like them, they can be a distraction. If you have tattoos, do the best you can to not draw attention to them in what you wear.

Piercings: Piercings are popular with some people in our culture but they can be a distraction to others. Take all piercings out except ears. If your ears are pierced, wear small diamonds or small earrings while presenting at your Parties.

Car: Make sure your car is clean on the inside and out. Don't have a car full of clothes, old sacks of food, or ashes in the ash tray. Never show up at a Party with a messy car.

Watch: Your watch tells a lot about you. Don't wear a cheap watch. Make getting a good watch a priority.

For women: If you are big boned or over weight, don't wear tight fitting clothes. Don't wear too many clothes when you are overweight. Wear some lip color. Wear nice accessories. People look at what you are wearing. Don't wear accessories that are cheap looking. Only wear fine perfume.

Handbag: Make sure you take only a small handbag. A big bulky, beat up handbag is a distraction. What's in your handbag is a reflection of your mind.

WATCH YOUR IMAGE-WOULD YOU BUY FROM YOU?

WATCH YOUR IMAGE-WOULD YOU JOIN YOU?

Step up your **image**
Step up **your** image
Step **up** your image
Step up your image
Step up your **image**
Step up **your** image
Step **up** your image
Step up your image
Step up your **image**
Step up **your** image
Step **up** your image
Step up your image
Step up your **image**
Step up **your** image
Step **up** your image
Step up your image

Top Formula = P.Q.S. Prospecting Quick System

When you find a successful formula or system, use it over and over again. Here is a formula to use when prospecting for Party Hosts. This information is *key* to success. Here are the quick steps to connect with a prospect you don't even know:

1: Create the prospect by making them realize a need.
2: Make the first impression impressive.
3: Get an interview by asking to get their information on how to reach them.
4: Arouse interest.

It's exciting when you have 100 distributors all out holding Parties on the SAME day!

I Will Persist Until I Succeed

"The prizes of life are at the end of each journey, not near the beginning; and it is not given to me to know how many steps are necessary in order to reach my goal. Failure I may still encounter at the thousandth step, yet success hides behind the next bend in the road. Never will I know how close it lies unless I turn the corner... I will persist until I succeed."

-Og Mandino

Posture Do And Don'ts During Your Parties

How you stand tells a lot about your confidence. Be aware of how you are standing when you present. **Here are some tips:**

- Stand up straight with your feet slightly apart and your arms ready to gesture.
- Lean slightly toward your guest.
- Don't lean on a table or on the back of a chair.
- Don't stand with your hands on your hips.
- Don't sway back and forth.
- Don't stand with your arms folded over your chest.
- Don't stand with your arms behind your back.
- Don't bury your hands in your pockets.

Gesture Do's And Don'ts During Your Parties

You want to use your hands. Keep your hands busy. **Here are some tips:**

- Create opportunities to use gestures. *"On the one hand... On the other hand..."*
- Vary your gestures.
- Make bold gestures.
- Gesture with authority.

Gestures That Don't Work At Parties

These gestures distract from your presentation.

- **The bug collector:** Don't pull or pick at the hair on the back of your neck or head. Looks like you might have bugs.
- **The kid in the room:** Don't play with what is in your hands, pens, markers, pointers, small pieces of paper. Rustling a piece of paper, candy wrapper, playing with your glasses, are all annoying to the guests.
- **The hygienist:** Don't rub your hands together like you are washing them. There is no soap or water or even a sink nearby.
- **The beggar:** Don't thrust your hands toward the audience like you are begging for something.
- **The lonely lover:** Don't hug yourself.
- **The proud own of jewelry:** Don't fiddle with your jewelry. Ring twisters are annoying presenters.
- **The tailor:** Don't fiddle with your clothing. Don't twist your tie or pinch it or rub it. No one will listen to you. The guest will wonder if you will end up choking yourself.
- **The optician:** Don't constantly adjust your glasses.
- **The banker:** Don't keep rattling coins in your pockets.

Section 3

Powerful Tools To Increase Your Business....

The Benefits Of Holding Parties

Sell the benefits of *why* people should schedule Parties. Put this list in a binder or folder or keep it by your phone so that you can list all the benefits of being associated with you and your opportunity.

Distributor Benefits:

✔**You bond** more effectively with people when you are with them.

✔**You can be competitive** and win prizes within your company.

✔**You get** a greater opportunity for getting add on sales.

✔**You get** a Host that is your business partner who does half your work for you by getting the customers there.

✔**You get** an opportunity to "*work the room*."

✔**You get** to practice new ideas.

✔**You get** to present your products and opportunity to several people at one time.

✔**You get** to show guests how easy the business is.

✔**You get** higher sales for your time invested as compared to a booth or door to door or other sales events.

✔**You get** to be creative.

✔**You get** to schedule more Parties.

✔**You get** to do on the job training for anyone who wants to join your opportunity.

✔**You get** to go for greatness.

✔**You get** to have a captive audience.

✔**You get** to give dad or mom private one on one time with the children parenting at home.

✔**You get** to introduce either company specials or make up your own.

✔**You get** to share your enthusiasm.

✔**You get** share the products and the opportunity over and over.

✔**You get** your Host to introduce you to NEW people. You don't have to pay an advertising fee.

✔**You get** to have a fun break away from your own home responsibilities and parenting.

Add:

Guest Benefits:

✔**You get** a night out.

✔**You get** great new decorating ideas.

✔**You get** house warming ideas.

✔**You get** to ask questions of and hear a presentation from a knowledgeable distributor.

✔**You get** to avoid traffic, crowded stores and long checkout lines.

✔**You get** to experience a Party as a reason to get friends together that you never see otherwise.

✔**You get** to have fun.

✔**You get** to Host a Party to give the opportunity to help your friends by sharing products that you believe in.

✔**You get** to learn product tips you would never get from a catalog.

✔**You get** to make new friends.

✔**You get** to see, touch and experience OPENED products before purchasing.

✔**You get** to shop from the safety and comfort of your own home.

✔**You get** to shop from your seat, not on your feet.

✔**You get** to try out new recipes and share cooking secrets.

Add:

Schedule 52 Parties A Year ONE A Week Is The Goal

The goal is to have at LEAST one Party a week. Do not let up or stop working until you schedule at least one Party a week. Work on getting Parties scheduled the first 2 weeks of the month.

Here is how: Send out *The Booking Letter*. You want everyone in your successline doing this in January EVERY YEAR. Start reminding and training about this no later than early November. (see page 61)

Start here: Begin a list of people who you think might be interested in having a Party. Use *The Booking Letter* below as a place to start to write your own letter. The idea is to have *The Booking Letter* ready to send out on December 23-24 on colored paper with no other literature along with it. It is to arrive at the potential Host home in the mail between the 25th and the end of the year.

Do this: By January 3rd, it's time to focus on scheduling Parties.

The Fortune Is In The Follow Up

The more letters you send out, the more chances you have to book lots of Parties for the rest of the year. When you do, that gives you a boost to start your year. Follow up. Follow up and then follow up again.

Idea: Use this letter every year for 3-5 years straight and **follow up, and schedule a Party a week.**

Important: Get trained on how to present your product **AND** your opportunity.

Note: *The Booking Letter* is **ONLY** for those who are determined to book 52 Parties a year and are committed to doing so. Before you start to tackle this, make sure you are committed, have your calendar, your script and are ready to build a business in Party Plan. It takes persistence, focus, and follow up. A fortune awaits those of you who do this and who teach others in your successline to do the same.

Spend One Day A Week Scheduling Parties

Take one day every week doing nothing but calling prospects who would like to have a Party with you. It takes dedication and focus, but once you have it going, *it's like a train that has left the station.*

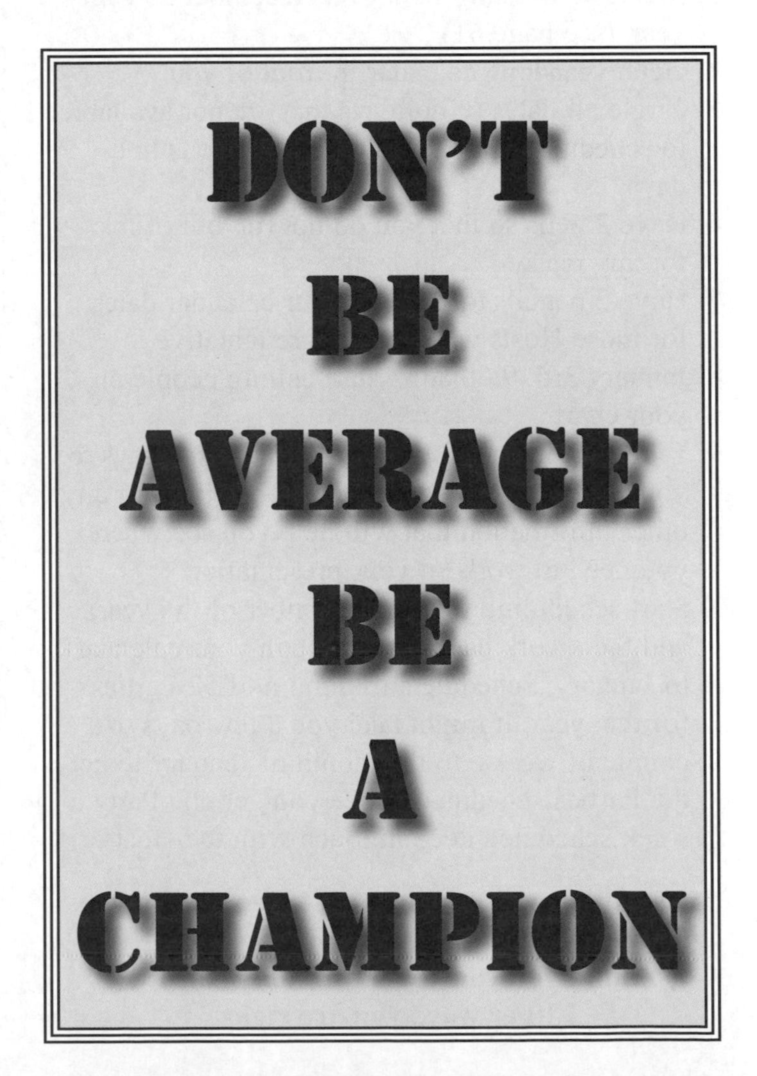

10 Tips On How To Use The Booking Letter

1. Make a list of who you send the letter to. The Headings are: Name: Date Called: Reached, Yes/No: Interested in becoming a distributor: Yes/No: Scheduled Party: Not a good time: Please call another time: Referrals: Notes:

2. Print that list out and put the list in a manila folder or write the list of names and phone numbers in a spiral notebook. Use your own system.

3. Mail *The Booking Letter* on December 23 every year. (see page 61)

4. Get a year-long calendar in front of you.

5. Circle all dates of holidays that are not available to schedule a Party. Example: Religious holidays.

6. Have 2 pens so that you do not run out of ink for any reason.

7. Have 2 pencils to write in your calendar dates for those Hosts whose dates are tentative.

8. January 3rd: 9:00 a.m., start calling people on your chart.

9. Take copious notes on what each person says to you. Pay attention to attitudes, objections or any other information that will help you see where you need to work on your presentation.

10. Start scheduling first in December of the year, and then work backward through your calendar to January. Schedule a minimum of 52 Parties for the year. It might take you a few days to a couple of weeks, to the month of January to get the Parties scheduled. Once you get one Party a week scheduled keep in touch with the Hosts.

If you think you can use this letter to help you grow your business, you probably can. If you think you can't you probably can't. Either way...you are right.

Testimonial From Val Sowa

"In 2003, I was determined to succeed in Party Plan. I used the ***exact*** *version of this letter, only changing my name, my stats and the specials I offer my customers every year. I made a plan to follow up - 20 calls a day for 15 days. The letter went out on December 23. I began following on January 3. With relative ease I booked 52 Parties–1 Party a week for 52 weeks. Even better, some customers* ***called me*** *to book dates, some emailed me their dates and some even circled their preference and mailed it back to me. I sent everyone a postcard to confirm their date and confirmed again the month before their Party. People couldn't believe that I booked that far in advance, but when I told them there was a chance that I would run out of dates, they readily got out their planners. I am a firm believer that people want what they fear not having. By holding and verbalizing the belief that you will fill up your calendar, you create a sense of immediacy for the people who want to work with you. Utilizing this one simple tool allowed me to focus on building my personal team, promoting leaders and helping everyone else be successful. By December of 2003, because of my incredible year, I had 15 home Parties dated and reserved for January, 2004. Prior to sending out my booking letter for 2004."* - **Val Sowa**, Discovery Toys, USA

Note: This letter works. All you do is send it out and follow up. Be prepared for lots of *"no's"* and a few *"yes's"*.

THE BOOKING LETTER

Dear Customer (or better yet, their name):

Happy holidays! Thank you for an incredible year. I am a (your title) with (your company). Because of people like you, my team sales were over (put amount, for example $50,000–whatever that amount is) in product this year.

I'm part of an organization that really cares about customer service. Satisfying your needs and wants is our top priority. So when you think of (your company name) think of me and not of running to a local store. I am only a phone call away. My number is (phone number). You are important and valuable to me. Serving you is my business. I love what I do. Being a representative for (your company name) has been such a huge benefit to my family and me this year. It's been a perfect part-time job for me. I absolutely love what I do. This is my career. After the first of the year, I'll be calling you to see if you would like to schedule a Party with me. Here's how that would benefit you (list all the benefits).

We will be partners for your Party. You get the people there, and I will do the rest. If you would rather, just mail the enclosed form back to me, that will be fine too. If I don't hear right back from you, I'll give you a quick call in the next two weeks to schedule your Party.

Here are my available dates for Parties this year: Please circle your first and second choices:

January: 8,9,10,11,16,17,18,22,23, 24,25,29, 30, 31
February: 5,6,7,8, 9,11,12,13,15,19,20,21,22,27,28
March: 4,5,6,11,12,13,14,26,27,28
April: 2,3,4,8,9,20,11,12,15,16,17,18,22,23,24,25,29
May: 1,2,3,6,7,8,12,13,14,15,16,17,20,23,24,27,28,29
June: 2,3,4,5, 10,11,12,16,17,18,19,20,23,24,28,29,30
July: 1,5,6,7,8,12,13,14,18,19,20
August: 4,5,6,7,8,9,12,13,18,19,20,22,23,24,25,26
September: 1,2,3,4,5,6,7,8,9,10,11,12,13,14,15,16,17,18,19,20,21,22,23,24,25,26,27
October: 1,2,3,4,5,6,7,8,9,10,11,12,13,14,15,16,17,18,19,20,21,22,23,24,25,26,27,28
November: 1,2,3,4,5,6,7,8,9,10,11,12,13,14,15,16,17,18,19,20,21,22,23,24,25,26, 27
December: 1,2,3,4,5,6,7,8,9,10,12,13,14,15,16,17,18

As always, when you are one of my customers, you benefit even more, because you can always buy my product at 10-15% (or whatever you choose) discount all year long. This is going to be a great year! I appreciate your business so much. I look forward to being your (your company name) sales representative. Thanks in advance. I'm looking forward to having a conversation with you in the next couple of weeks. Have your first and second choices marked and have your calendar ready. *I'll be calling you soon.*

Happy Holidays, (your name)

The key to getting multiple bookings at a Party for more Parties is to...

Perk up your presentation!

Important: Work on your presentation skills. Learn what to say from your Upline or someone in your company who is getting results.

Idea: When you follow up on *The Booking Letter* (see page 61) in January, schedule Parties for the following December, November, October, September, then August, and continue on backwards in the year. Many people can't think about having a Party soon after the holidays but can commit to one way out. This relieves pressure. **Then:** When you begin to your Parties in April and May and say: *"I am booked for the rest of the year."* You will get many more recruits! Try it!

During the day say to yourself no matter what mood you are in:
Happy, Happy, Happy

Using Post Cards

Send out postcards and discover which postcard draws the most interest. Then you will know which benefit will spark interest in selling coming to a Party or in joining the business. Know each benefit until you find the one or two benefits that consistently give you massive returns on your investment. The good thing about this testing is that you will get lots of prospects while you are testing. Example:

- **How to get a new car every two years and never make a single car payment again. Come to my Party on (date) and see what's involved.**
- **How to earn $500+ extra every week without leaving your home. Come to my Party on (date) and see how you can get started right away.**
- **Meet positive new friends while networking with fellow part-time business entrepreneurs.**
- **Start a part-time business that will pay off your new home mortgage. Come to Suzie's Party and hear how.**
- **Trade two hours of television time to learn how your neighbors are collecting an extra check every month. Come to John's Party and find out how you can too.**

Make your headlines to attract a certain prospect. Continue to invite! Invite, Invite, Invite, Invite!

THE DAY YOU TAKE COMPLETE RESPONSIBILITY FOR YOURSELF, THE DAY YOU STOP MAKING EXCUSES, THAT'S THE DAY YOU START YOUR PATH TO THE TOP.

Canisters/Lead Boxes

Make it enticing for people in your area to want to take the time to fill in the tear-off sheet. You can be brand new. Flyers and canisters work great.

1: Get a dozen shoeboxes or small cans.

2: Take the lid off.

3: Tape a portion or all of the front cover from your catalog on the box.

4: Put a sticker on the cover of the catalog that says: **DRAWING FOR** (prize) **of** (your company name) **prize to be given away on** (select a date 2 weeks from the time you plan to give the prizes away).

5: Make some note pads 3 x 5 that say: (Make certain that your name and phone number are on the pads of tear off sheets).

6: Take the canisters on your daily path to Doctors, Dentists, shoe cobbler, restaurants, etc. Ask if you can place the canisters in those places for a few days. Every few days, pick up your leads (so no one else will). On the day of the drawing dump ALL the leads together into one canister and draw out as many winners as you want and call the winners on the telephone enthusiastically.

Say: *"Today is your lucky day! You won the drawing for a FREE product from me! Here is what you just won (name product). Have you ever heard of (your company name)? I would love to meet with you to give you your FREE gift and to tell you more about our opportunity. When would be a good time, and where would you like to meet? Would you please bring a friend along so I can share the opportunity to both of you at the same time? If you do, you will get another FREE product! So, how does that sound?"* They will tell a zillion people about you. You have just opened a major new path to new customers and potential Hosts.

You also have all those leads collected. Do this enough and you will have people who will check off wanting to Host a Party for you and wanting information on how to join you! Be sure and follow *up every few days* with the leads you collect. This is a very effective and inexpensive way of collecting leads. Move canisters around town from time to time. Keep at least 12 out at all times. For years.

Party Plan is a word of mouth business. If you have an uncomplicated product to sell, if you have your own personal testimonial about the products, if your company delivers products and checks on time, all it takes is opening your mouth! Put out flyers, canisters, and send out *The Booking Letter*, (see page 61) get to some powerful trainings and your business will skyrocket! You are on your way!

TEAR OFF SHEETS

Interested in hosting a Home Party............☐

Interested in attending a Home Party.........☐

Interested in selling......................................☐

Interested in referring someone...................☐

NAME: ______________________________

Phone number: ______________________

Must be over 18 years old to enter drawing.

To reach me immediately call (your name):

(Your Phone Number)

Sample Flyer

Let everyone know that you are in business. You can't hang out a sign in front of a store, so you must let people know how to find you. Put flyers on Bulletin Boards, in with your bills, on windshields, and everywhere you can think of. Paper your town.

Creamcheese Products are now in this area!

Schedule a Home Party and you get (fill this in)

Call *Suzie* at: (your phone number) to schedule your Party today

Only 8 available dates per month left

It's easy for people to find you if you are willing to take the time to make flyers and paper your area!

Starting A New Area

Sometimes it can be very difficult to start holding Parties in a new area when you know no one and no one has heard of your company or products. The more people who know about your company, the better your business will be. Start with your own area, and blanket it. Paper your area with flyers. Put up flyers everywhere. Do as many Parties in one area as you can. Start spreading the news.

Booking Coupon

Hand this coupon out at your Parties and as you prospect. The idea is to get guests at Parties or others to think about giving you names to prospect for more Parties or to recruit.

Remember: STEAM

Let's Party

Bring a friend and **you get...**_______

Bring an outside order and **you get...**_______

Bring a friend who has been in **Sales** and **you get...**_______

Bring your child's favorite **Teacher** and **you get...**_______

Bring someone who is **Enthusiastic** and **you get...**_______

Bring someone who has a great **Attitude** and **you get...**_______

or needs extra **Money** and **you get...**_______

129 Ways To Prospect For Home Parties

Note: Some of these ideas may or may not work in your plan. You might have to make some adjustments or additions or deletions for your product and opportunity. Take the best, leave the rest.

1. Advertise in local programs for festivals, school plays, church Bazaars, etc.
2. Advertise in your alumni newsletter and/or local newspaper.
3. Advertise in your church bulletin.
4. Always have your business cards ready.
5. Ask past Hosts at Parties to talk about the benefits they have gotten from having Parties.
6. Ask friends to have a Party.
7. Ask friends to help you get started or reach a certain goal.
8. Ask your friends/family to help you get started.
9. ASK, ASK, ASK.
10. At the beginning of your presentation, mention the Host goal. *"Suzie wants you all to have a great time."*
11. Be friendly and enthusiastic but serious about scheduling more Parties.
12. Be prepared to answer questions about what you do.
13. Be willing to share the business opportunity every day.

Here is who to contact:

14. Anyone who has said *"maybe"* or *"sometime."*
15. At least 2 potential Hosts every night.
16. Past Hosts.
17. Potential Hosts who postponed or never booked. The timing might not have been right. If they decline again, ask for referrals.
18. People you know. Always ask first to schedule a Party for you and if not then ask for referrals.
19. Realtors with ideas for *"new home packages."*
20. Carry a note pad and pen to jot down names as you think of and meet prospects.
21. The Cerebral Palsy Association.
22. The Children with Learning Disabilities Association.
23. Churches, synagogues in their adult classes.
24. Colleges in your area–Community Colleges and Four Year Colleges, contact teachers/professors.
25. Car dealerships, make baskets of your products for people to see.
26. Nursery schools.
27. Schools. Start in the school districts that are more affluent.
28. Women's Clubs, literary, garden clubs, bridge clubs.
29. Co-workers, current friends.
30. Curriculum supervisors or people in charge of special programs in school districts are often interested in fundraisers.

32\. Day Care Providers Association. Get president's phone number from the local NAEYC. (They have lists of organizations in your area.)

32\. Describe and highlight the Host plan during your Parties. Put it on Poster board.

33\. Do benefits for various clubs or groups.

34\. Do random mailings of invitations.

35\. Don't be timid talking about your products or prospecting in stores, parks, or countless other places. Strike up a conversation.

36\. Make calls to everyone you can think of.

37\. Make it a point to encourage frequent customers to regularly plan Parties.

38\. Encourage Hosts to reschedule shows as soon as new brochures or campaigns start.

39\. Encourage relatives to book a Party.

40\. Encourage your Hosts and guests to refer potential Hosts to you. Always ask for referrals.

41\. Follow through on every booking lead.

The fortune is in the follow up.

42. Follow-up phone calls to particularly interested guests.
43. Get a list from Welcome Wagon in your neighborhood.
44. Put up flyers everywhere in your community.
45. Put canisters out. (see page 63)
46. Give a catalog to the receptionist at your doctor's or dentist's office.
47. Give extra service and time to good customers.
48. Give products as gifts or donations.
49. Going through directors of nursery schools or parents with children in nursery schools often leads to demonstrations or fundraisers for these groups.
50. Have a booth at a school fair or Octoberfest.
51. Have a coffee and ask the parents of your children's classrooms to pop by.
52. Have a T-shirt made up for yourself and team that says "*ask me about* (your company)" and for your children. Wear it!
53. Have the Hosts tell why they decided to Host a Party. Hold an open house with the Host in addition to the Party at a different time.
54. Have a Party on your driveway, borrow your friends' driveways, set up a table and put out a banner saying you are there.
55. Have your spouse or partner or friends promote the products at work. Call them your Ambassadors.
56. Hold a Holiday Shopping Party for parents.
57. Hold an opportunity night in your community.
58. Hold one Party yourself for a group of friends and contacts. Their enthusiasm helps insure a good turnout for your first bookings.
59. Hold 52 Parties and continue to encourage future bookings.
60. Hold your own open house with products displayed, and invite lots of people.
61. Host a Party before or during a PTA meeting.
62. Host an office Party or brunch.
63. If you have a baby, be sure to have some of your catalogs in your stroller. Babies often draw comments and could lead to new customers.
64. Include a coupon for a special discount in your booking letter.
65. Include a flyer with your bill payments.
66. Keep a list of special requests and let those guests know when that product is on sale.
67. Leave your business cards on bulletin boards or at local businesses.
68. La Leche League Meetings are packed with prospects. This is a League for mothers who nurse their babies for over one year.
69. Let guests keep a catalog or sales brochure to keep or pass around work.
70. Local newspapers are a good place to advertise.
71. Mail out samples and catalogs to friends.
72. Make contacts with groups who are looking for free speakers.
73. Mention Host gifts and other benefits at least 3 times per Party.
74. Mention how much your *"average"* Host gets in (your Host plan).
75. Mothers of Twins Club, get information from a local hospital.
76. National Associations for the Education of Young Children (NAEYC). Contact Universities and ask for and National Associations, local chapter president, secretary, etc.
77. Never walk by a young parent with a baby without complimenting how beautiful the baby is. Have your business card ready to hand them.
78. New people may be looking for a distributor in your area. Let them know what you do.
79. Offer a bonus for Hosts who schedule on days and/or months you need an extra Party.
80. Offer a bridal registry/birthday club.
81. Offer holiday wish lists to your guests and then

call the gift giver and tell him what the guests wants.

82. Offer to do a class for your local grocery store.
83. Open a phone book and randomly choose companies to call on. A=Automobile dealerships, B=Boat companies, etc.
84. Parents without partners are a great people to have Parties with, nice way to meet new people for singles.
85. Participate in a school fund-raiser.
86. Put a catalog in the employee lunchroom at local businesses. Make sure your name and how to reach you are on every single piece of literature you hand out.
87. Put a catalog in the teacher's lounge at your child's school.
88. Post flyers where the public can see them.
89. Promote baby showers if you have products that would be terrific for babies or parents.
90. Promote Bridal Parties.
91. Put a poster in the window of a children's clothing manufacturer outlet.
92. Put an "*ask me about* (company name)" button on your handbag or coat.
93. Put catalogs at a nursery school so parents can take them when they come to pick up their children.
94. Put current catalog in your neighbor's door.
95. Put flyers under windshield wipers.
96. Put flyers out on your daily path, shoe repair, hair stylist, manicurist, etc.
97. Put flyers around your neighborhood.
98. Read sales, self-improvement, and positive thinking books to find better words to use.
99. Resources: Always ask *"Who do you know who might be interested?"*
100. Review orders from past Parties-guests who have bought frequently, a certain type of item, etc.
101. Send a catalog to a co-worker that has moved.
102. Send a catalog to other distributors you know.
103. Senior Citizen Clubs. Call Senior Citizen Homes to find these clubs. There are people playing bridge, going to Book Clubs, Investment Clubs, golfing together who might be interested in your products.
104. Set up a display at a craft fair.
105. Set up a display at a mall.
106. Set up products at garage sales, flea markets, teacher meetings, booths, etc. This gives great exposure and leads to contacts.
107. Share upcoming specials at Parties and during phone calls. Invite your friends be the first to see and try your new products at *their* next Party.
108. Smile when talking on the phone. It will show through.
109. Special Education Associations. If you have educational toys, books or games, contact these Associations for leads of who is responsible for purchasing their educational products.
110. Spend time every day prospecting looking for new business.
111. Start an e-mail address book of customers who want to know what the monthly specials are. Always mention the Host specials. If there isn't one, create one.
112. Suggest hosting a Party to do holiday shopping without leaving home.
113. Take a catalog to all social meetings.
114. Talk about upcoming specials with everyone.
115. Tell your Host how much they saved by having a Party. They may decide to become a distributor.
116. Some restaurants have fish bowls where they ask customers to put their business cards. Once a week they draw a business card from the bowl and the lucky winner gets a FREE

lunch. Ask the owner of the restaurant if you can give away a FREE product as well a week if you can have those business cards. Follow up and prospect those whose business card that you collect.

117. Treat Hosts to a special *"Host Appreciation Tea or Coffee"* at your home or at a lovely location.
118. Use Host flyers. Use postcards and/or newsletters to continue to spark interest.
119. Use questions, when prospecting. Interested is interesting.
120. Use your products and samples at home, office, camping, Parties, etc.
121. Write down names of people who would benefit from Hosting a Party, then call them.
122. YMCA or YWCA, put up sign in lobby.
123. You want to ask, *"My company has given me the responsibility to find five key people urgently in this area who would be interested in being a part time representative. Who do you know, where do they live, how can I reach them?"*
124. Your products make a difference. Share the benefits. What benefit is it to the customer to own your products over others? Study the benefits, memorize them so that you can sell more product.
125. Your local library. Frequent there and look for prospects. Readers are leaders.
126. Your doctors, dentists, attorneys, coaches, teachers all know people. Ask for referrals.
127. You are standing in lines, take the time to prospect those around you.
128. Your grocery stores, coffee houses, book stores all have people in them who know people.
129. Your are you own best advertisement, use your mouth. Use your own products. Be a walking billboard.

There's
a lot of sale
in a puppy
dogs tail

Presentation Ideas

☑**Poster Boards:** Pictures are worth a 1,000 words. It's not what you know, it's what you show. Posters save time. Shave off seconds from your presentation so that you can maximize your time. Set up FAST, do a presentation that gets results, take orders and leave. If you have products that are easy to glue onto poster boards do so. You can do a quick presentation in 15-20 minutes by showing the poster boards. Use your samples for this. Invest in extra samples if you need to.

☑**Catalogs:** If you have catalogs, cut out photos and glue them onto poster boards and place around the room at the Party. Makes your products a lot easier to show.

☑**Trips:** Glue photos of your incentive trips onto giant poster boards and take them to your Parties. Show what is possible to earn besides money.

☑**Car:** If you have earned a car, take a photo of it and glue it onto giant poster board. Place it for all to see what is possible to earn.

☑**Free Products:** If you get free products for being a distributor at any level, take photos of the products and glue them on poster boards to place around your Party.

☑**Bucket Brigade:** Make up buckets of products for people to buy and carry out.

☑**Baskets:** Have every kind of holiday basket made up with the price on the basket. Put 6-7 products in a basket, and make one with 5-6 products in it for sale at the Party.

☑**Build your own bucket or basket:** Take an extra few baskets and tell guests that if they buy 6-7 or more products *they will get* a free basket to keep their purchases in.

☑**Cash and Carry baskets:** Where you take orders at your Party, break apart inventory items that come several to a pack. Figure the total cost of the item including tax and shipping and divide that cost by the number of single items it becomes. Mark each item accordingly. This is a great way for your guests to take home something from the Party.

☑**2 of a kind:** Take 2 brand new boxed products from inventory to your Party. **Say:** *"I only have 2 (product names) left. I did a Party last night and (a number) were grabbed up, now I only have these 2 with me today."* People always want something they think is in short supply.

☑**Keep your Party display simple:** If you have your products in containers you can present your product right out of your containers. **Say:** *"We have had so much fun tonight, I can come back next week and show you more!"*

☑**Don't present the products Party:** Let your guests all grab a product and demonstrate it. Keep your Parties so simple that anyone will see they can do what you are doing.

☑**Look What I've Won Album:** Start a photo album from the FIRST time you earn ANYTHING from your company. Keep all recognition cards, letters, etc. in this album. Include photos of you with your Upline, your successline, and your mentors with you. Include photos on your incentive trips. **Sell YOU, *not your company*!**

☑**Star Search Album:** Have an album with your leaders photos in it. Include a blank page and **say**: *"Can you see your photo here?"* on it. Call it *"My Star Search"* album. People will want to be included. Paint the picture that they could be considered one of your leaders.

☑**10 of a Kind:** Plan to sell 10 of one kind of product at a Party. Focus on selling the benefits of that product. This can greatly increase sales.

The Bamboo Tree

Have you ever seen a Bamboo Tree? It soars over a hundred feet straight up. What's even more awesome about a Bamboo Tree, though, is how one grows. First, you have to get a Bamboo stock, about 18 inches long. Dig a hole 3 feet deep, and bury the stock completely in the ground. For the next 5 years, that stock must be watered every single day, 365 days a year. If one day is missed the tree will never appear. But, if meticulous care is taken for that 5 years, it is said that on that 1,825th day, the ground will break open and the tree will appear out of the ground.What happens next is the phenomenon of the Bamboo Tree. The tree will soar to over 90 feet in a matter of 6 weeks! It grows at a rate of 3 feet every 24 hours. You could practically sit back and watch it grow. Some people say it takes 6 weeks for a Bamboo Tree to grow, while others say it takes 5 years and 6 weeks to grow. I guess it depends on if you were the one watering it for 5 years. Imagine if you were to plant a Bamboo Tree in your backyard, and went out every day to water it, rain or shine. Suppose one of your neighbors sees you doing this for several days and asks, *"What are you watering the same spot of ground every day for?"*. You reply, *"I'm growing a Bamboo Tree. You water it every day for 5 years, then it grows to 90 feet in 6 weeks. You ought to try it."* He ponders the idea, then replies, *"No, I think I'll wait and see if yours works."* The next year, that same neighbor sees that your still watering the spot of ground. He asks, *"Why are you still watering that spot and nothing happens?"* You tell the man, *"It takes time to grow a Bamboo Tree, but once it comes out of the ground, it is the most awesome sight to see. You ought to grow one too!"* The neighbor just laughs and replies, *"No, I'll just wait to see how yours turns out."* The third year, the neighbor isn't talking to you any more, and doesn't want anything to do with you. The whole neighborhood has heard about the crazy lady on the block that keeps watering this same spot in her yard, hoping to grow a Bamboo Tree. The fourth year, they're sizing you up for a straight jacket, and none of the children are allowed to play near your home. But in that fifth year, the ground breaks open, and that stock that you had planted catches it's first rays of sunshine, and away it goes! Six weeks later the neighbors are admiring this awesome sight that you now have, wishing they had a Bamboo Tree. But they would have to wait 5 years for theirs to grow! Boy, do they wish they would have listened to you 5 years ago. You have planted your stock in your Party Plan. It is much like a Bamboo Tree. It takes watering every day. You don't see much happen for sometime, but you keep watering it. Many people will ask you, *"How's your business going? Have you made your fortune yet? I'll wait to see how you do."* Then one day, your organization will open up, catch it's first rays of sunshine, and away it goes! You could practically sit back and watch it grow, faster and faster, higher and higher. While you're sitting on the top of your Bamboo Tree enjoying the view, others will be thinking, *"I wish I had listened, and planted my stock."* For a very small number of people that are super consultants, this could be within a few months. Others will work diligently for maybe 5 years (hopefully less) growing their Bamboo Tree. They will make mistakes, poor decisions, use poor judgment, even be discouraged at times and think about quitting, but, if they keep doing it, and be diligent in their watering, it will work! Keep it simple. It's a simple opportunity! Just like Party Plan...keep at it!

Never Give Up!! Go for greatness! Fire up!

Let's Party!

Section 4

Coach Your Host....

Be A Modern Distributor Select Host Carefully

You are up to date when you discover that being consistent is having *at LEAST* 4 Parties a month, and sharing your products and opportunity over and over again.

Be Picky With Whom You Schedule A Party

Work with the Host to make sure they understand your expectations and to be clear what is in it for them. If you kid yourself and think someone wants a Party with you and you have had to beg them to Host a Party for you, most likely they will cancel. Why not work with serious Hosts that value their time and yours? Explain to your Host what is entailed in having a Party and what your expectations are and make sure they understand what is involved, and what's in it for them.

Here is what's in it for you: If you help the Hosts get what they want, they will spread the word about you and your products and opportunity.

Coaching Your Host

Don't assume Hosts understand what they are to do to have a successful Party.

Say to future Host: *"Have you ever had a Party in home? If you have not, you are in for a treat because I am going to coach you on how to have a successful Party. If you will let me help, you can have a fantastic Party."*

Check Off List

Give the Host a check off list that includes Party information: Time: Date: Payment: Dress: How long the Party will last: and can they count on you to attend?

Maximize Your Time Educate The Host

Take the time to coach your Host on how to have a fantastic Party. Preparation is 99% of all success and much of Party plan. This takes some time, but the results will sparkle and shine for both you the distributor and the Host. Without coaching the Host, you are leaving the results up to chance. Preparation breeds productivity.

Start With The Outcome Of The Party

1. **What's in it for the Host** to have a Party with you?
2. **Dedicate yourself** to making sure that the Host has a successful Party.
3. **Let your Host know** how important they are to the success of the Party.
4. **Say to the Host:** *"We are going to partner together to make your Party a great success. Your part of the partnership is to get the people there. My part of the partnership is to show up, give a presentation, get you (Host plan), schedule more Parties and recruit others to do the same, get everyone's products to them when I say I will and create some fun."*

Who has the bigger part of the partnership? The distributor, of course. You get paid to present, sell products and teach others to do the same. Results come from those who use these words. You must get the Host to understand that they must get the people there. That's their only job.

Next...

Decide what do *you* need to accomplish by being the distributor at the Party?

Follow-Up/Over Booking

Work on getting...

No Cancellations

You must make it clear with your Host that you are like a doctor or dentist, that if they cancel, you can't reschedule that Party right away. Be clear that your income depends on them following through, being responsible, being dependable and Hosting the Party. *You must* follow up with the Host several times, asking how they are doing on contacting their guests and how many people they are expecting. *You must* call the day before and the day of the Party. You cannot show up, and there is no Party and be devastated. That would be YOUR fault for assuming. You must follow up. Over schedule if you have to. If you have to do two Parties a day to make the money you need, do it. Make sure you keep in close contact with the Host. Don't assume they will hold the Party. Make them so excited about having the Party that THEY are excited to hold it.

Here is why: If you double schedule shows and if the first Party is a for sure go, you can always give the other Party away to someone in your successline and when you do: **Say:** *"Today is your Lucky Day! I have a Party that I can't do. Would you like to partner with me and do the Party? Here is what I have in mind, you keep the money, all future Parties and recruits from the Party and I get the sales value towards a trip I am working toward. Or you get the sales value and I get the rest. Which way works better for you?"*

> ***Some people have thousands of reasons why they cannot do what they want to, when all they need is one reason why they can.***
>
> **-Dr. Jozsef Telkes, Hungary**

Make Sure You Are Clear What Is In It For The Host

Hosts want FREE or discounted products, gifts, recognition or significance that give *them* value. Distributors are required by today's competitive conditions to treat the Party Plan as a business of education about *why* the products and opportunity will work and serve the guest.

Dedicate Yourself To Making The Party A Giant Success

Dedicate your effort to the Host. An important factor in gaining the fired up frame of mind and keeping it, which is basic to success in Party Plan, is to dedicate yourself to your Host, honestly putting *their* interests first...doing your best for them...looking at things from their point of view...and selling from their point of view.

What are the 2 words every Host wants to hear?

I am committed to your success

You Get

Why Dedicate Yourself To The Host

Everyone carries on continuously within, a kind of moral bookkeeping. Distributors are the same in this respect as everyone else. When you dedicate yourself to your Host's best interests, you build up within yourself a *"moral credit balance."* It puts you in an expectant, hopeful frame of mind so necessary to Party Plan success. You feel you have something good coming to you. It puts an end to the inner feelings of guilt that keep so many distributors ineffectual. The distributors who do things only for their own advantage, then try to kid themselves and the Host that it is being done for their sake will not build a long, lasting business. Keep your word to your Host. Build trust based on your honesty and they will do business with you for years.

Encourage Outside Orders

Prior to the Party get plenty of catalogs or your website to the Host so they can collect outside orders that count toward their Party. Coach your Host to give catalogs to invited guests who cannot make it to the actual Party. Tell those guests to place their order prior to the Party so that the Host can include it for the upcoming Party. It's very exciting for a Host to have several hundred dollars in orders prior to the actual Party. Encourage outside orders.

Need to Succeed

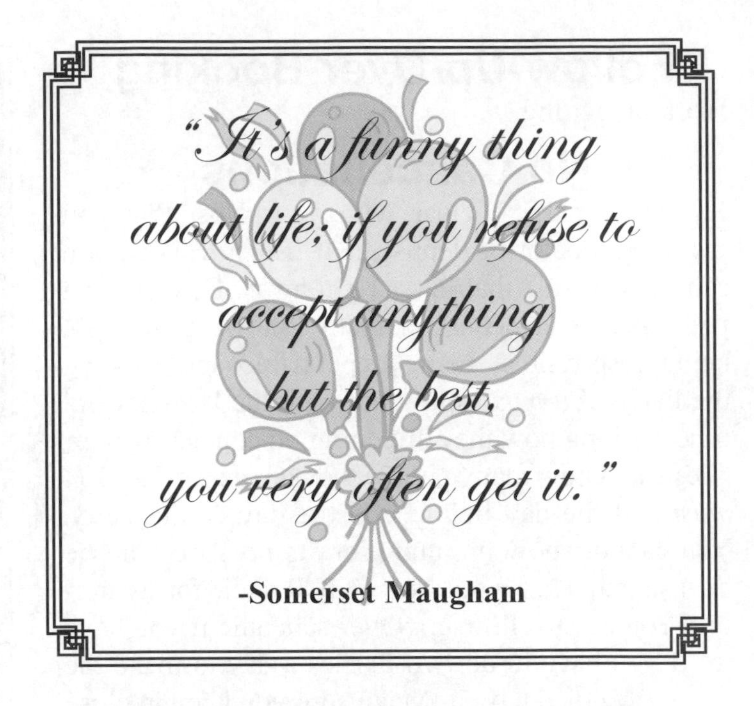

The More We Sell At *Your* Party, The More *You Get*

Keep in the front of the Host's mind *what is in it for them.* The more guests they get to their Party, the higher the sales, the higher the sales, the more benefit to the Host. Keep telling the Host that. Keep encouraging them to invite more guests to their Party.

Have Inventory Available For Impulse Buyers

Have a basket or box of inventory at your Parties. As people arrive, direct them to this box. Mark it 30%–50% off and have it available for those who are impulse buyers or who have need for it at that time. Perhaps they are in need of a gift the next day and can't wait for their products to be delivered. Don't miss a sale. Always have a minimum of $200 in products in your personal inventory to take with you to all Parties.

My $1,000+ Party

Story Time: One year I had a Party with a close friend Phillis in Dallas, Texas in HER home. Phillis invited 20 guests and asked them all to bring 2 friends. Most did. As I stood at the door, guests were coming in and even though I had a badge on with my name on it saying I was the distributor, many thanked ME for having them to a Party in MY home. They didn't even know who the Host was! The Party was well over $1,000, everyone had a terrific time. ***I made the guests want all of my products!*** I scheduled 8 Parties and got 9 potential recruits. It's all about working with your Host. Phillis got all the FREE toys she wanted for her holiday presents and all the birthday presents for the following year. She was thrilled. The guests had a great time, and I got a ton of business. Phillis had many more Parties for me.

Work With Your Host About Children At The Parties vs. No Children

Absolutely no children unless they are babies under 3 months old. It's very difficult to control children. They are children. It's annoying to the distributor or a parent to be *shhhhhhhshing*...their children during the presentation. It's hard to talk over a cooing or screaming child. Children can knock over your products without meaning to and they can cause havoc. Some are boisterous and can be distracting to others. We all think our children are perfect but to others, they don't see them that way. It's best to leave them with a spouse, partner or baby sitter.

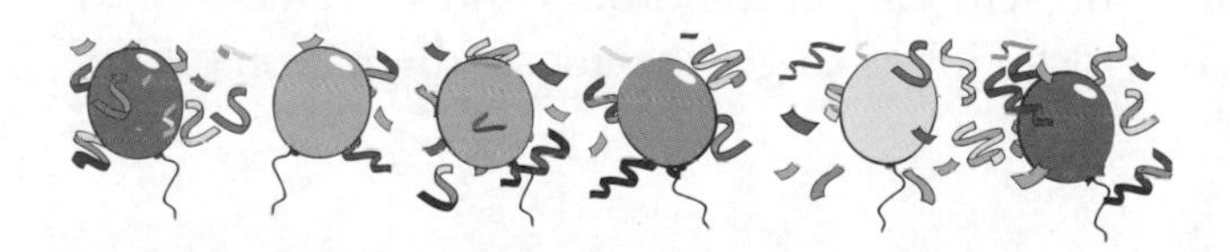

Taking Your Own Children To Parties

If you have a nursing baby, take the baby with you for the first three months only. Do not take toddlers with you under any circumstances to Parties in other people's homes. When your children are 13 years old, it's nice to take them with you, pay them a little bit to help carry in products, to sit quietly through your presentation and to help carry out products. This is only if your 13 year old is well behaved, of course. I found going to the Parties without children was less complicated. Let your Host know you are bringing your baby. Never surprise the Host.

It's Not What You Know, It's What You Show

Many guests are visual, and they want to SEE what Party Plan is all about. Remember, it's not what you know, it's what you *show that will reap you the most rewards*.

I know I am making progress, because I am making new mistakes.

Host Your Own Party

Hold your own Party. Invite people who have told you they are uninterested in having their own Party but would be interested in attending a Party. Follow up and call people. Now!

Story Time: One time, I sent out 80 catalogs with a written invitation on every catalog. No one came the day of the Party. The next day, I got on the phone and called the top 8 people who I really thought would have come and told them they had *"Missed a great Party and that I was going to leave my product display up for 2 more days so they could pop by and shop."* I didn't tell anyone that no one had come to the Party. They had all seen the catalog, but had missed the written invitations and were so sorry that they had not come to the Party. I sold $800 to those 8 who came the next day. Turn lemons into lemonade. Do not be slowed down. If something doesn't work, try another strategy. If nothing works, it's not the product, it's not the system, it's not the Pay Plan, it's not the area you live in, it's not the information in books and seminars you learn, it's something you need to change about you.

F.A.Y.C. - Think Of The Host

When you **F**orget **A**bout **Y**ourself **C**ompletely. WANT the Host to have a great experience working with you so think of the benefit for *them*. Come from contribution, always asking yourself: *"How can I help the Host get what they want?"* **Here is how:** Ask yourself, *"How can I make this the best Party for this Host?"* When you honestly dedicate your efforts to your Host's best interests, it puts the enormous power of right on your side, and immediately fills your mind with the expectation of good to come.

> **I am so proactive that I am pre-active.**

Have People Lined Up To Have Parties With You

Can you imagine, a line of guests ready to schedule a Party with you at your Party? If you can imagine it, get a vision of it, desire it and work on your skills, it will happen. If you give a fun, fast paced, interesting presentation, give plenty of significance to the Host, take all the orders, keep it uncomplicated, get the Host benefits that others can see or hear about, leave before being there too long, and you will have others interested in scheduling Parties with you. If you have a product that will benefit others, that others WANT to own, that's EASY to present you have a fantastic chance of scheduling Party after Party. If you try to make your product complicated and that you are an expert that no one can duplicate, good luck on easily scheduling more Parties. Parties are based on a uncomplicated presentation and on the desire for your product and opportunity.

Assure The Host The Party Will Be Uncomplicated

The Party needs to be uncomplicated and easy to duplicate. Assure your Host that you will arrive on time, give a brief 20-30 minute presentation, and that you will collect the orders and take the money. The Host's job is to get the guests there, you will do the rest.

A Valuable Lesson

Story Time: On a Saturday before Easter, I held a Party where the Host wanted all the children to come in their Easter suits and dresses. It was very important to her. She hired a baby sitter and said the children could all play in her back yard.

What did I say? I advised against doing this. With children there, we are leaving the Party open to disaster.

How to handle this? The Host didn't believe that was true. She was determined to hold the Party her way, with children. I agreed, never having had experienced this before. I arrived and there were children everywhere, all adorable and all in their finest clothes. They were all under 7 years old. When we got ready to start the Party, most of the children wanted to play in the back yard and some clung to their mommy and would not be parted, some interrupted, some cried, one spilled grape juice on the Host's white carpet and it was generally a lost Party. *But* I carried on *until*...squeals of laughter, and screaming crying came from the back yard.

Next: One of the children had turned a water hose on and was dowsing the others in their finest clothes. Some of the boys were standing under the water hose, dripping wet. The mothers were upset, shaken, shocked, mad, and were grabbing their children, heading for the bathroom to dry them off. They left the Party without even saying goodbye, furious at the Host. Not a good scene. I was horrified and sure that it would sink my business. I knew that they would tell everyone to never hold a Party with me. I thought the worst. My positive self talk went bye bye.

Next: Most everyone left, no orders were placed and I was so disappointed. *But* I had learned a valuable lesson. Fortunately the Host placed her own order but did not get any FREE products. She apologized and said how sorry she was that she had not listened to me and been coachable.

The good news: This was one of the most valuable Parties I ever held because from that day on, I could share what happened with others who had similar ideas. Never again did a Host invite guests to bring their children. Use my story to inform Hosts of how a good intention can become disastrous.

Remember Your Products

Always pack your products in your car prior to departing for the Party. Make sure you take all necessary paperwork.

Story Time: While I was a single parent, I had to get a baby sitter. The children had not been left with more than 5 sitters their entire lives. If that. This particular babysitter was a woman highly recommended by a friend of mine. I had a Party scheduled across town and was expecting 10-20 people. It was at night and there was a lot of traffic. I fed, bathed and got the children ready for bed, the house was neat, and I was ready to go. The babysitter arrived and the children all went to the front door to see who this stranger was who was to watch them for a couple of hours while I left to do a Party. They were about 9,7, and 5 at the time. I had explained to them the situation and reassured them that they would be fine with this lady. And that I would be home soon.

Chaos breaks loose! When the woman entered our entryway, she opened her handbag to drop her car keys into her bag, and as she did, the light overhead caught a shining sharp instrument in her handbag which happened to be a big pair of scissors. She had another bag she brought in of needle work but the children didn't see that. Clayton starting *screaming* that she had a knife and was going to hurt him, he *grabbed* little Ashley, pulled her running to his bedroom, locked the door, got under his bed and would not open the door. Sarah raced into her room, slammed and locked the door wailing. Oh my! I *wanted to stay home*, but I **needed** to leave.

What had they seen? The poor woman showed me her scissors and her bag of needle work. I took her into the living room, turned on the TV for her and gave her the number where I would be holding the Party. There were no cell phones in those days. And I left. I worried about my children the whole way to the Party. I arrived at the Host's home, carried in the products, returned to my car to get the other products and to my horror realized that I had forgotten half of my samples! It had taken me almost 40 minutes in the traffic to get there. I was plainly not thinking right. Instead of 20 people arriving, over 30 arrived. I would have had such a better Party if I had more samples. But, the show must go on. I ended up selling $700 and scheduling 3 Parties, got a couple of recruits and shortened my presentation to less than 15 minutes. And left. I drove home not excited about what I had earned or the Party *but totally worried about my children.* When I got home the baby sitter was watching TV, knitting away. She said the children were the easiest she had ever sat for, that they had never reappeared the entire time I was gone. I said good night to the sitter. I then knocked on the bedroom doors and found they were all still awake. They all climbed in bed with me to sleep the rest of the night and held on to me for dear life all night. **I never left them with a sitter again.** From that day on, I scheduled all of my Parties to be held during the day when they were in school.

All things are hard 'til they get easy

-Joseph Meade Kelley

Remember The Date Of The Party

Story Time: I had garage sales frequently to help with the month to month expenses. Although I was earning more than most women in America by this time, I was over 6 figures in debt as a result of attorney's fee from my divorce. I had a mountain of bills to pay every month and creditors calling all of the time. From time to time, the children outgrew their clothes, toys, and stuffed animals. I was ready to sell things that I no longer wanted. I would THROW everything I didn't want or was tired of out into the garage. When the heap got over 4 to 5 feet tall, I would set up a metal table or two and would stay up all night if I had to and set up a garage sale. I would make Garage Sale signs to put up at both ends of my street directing people to my garage. One Saturday morning, in the summer, my children were gone for the day and I had planned a huge garage sale. This time, I put an advertisement in the paper. It was a scorching hot Texas summer morning. I was up early, put my hair into a ponytail, put on some shorts, a shirt and sandals and wore no makeup. At 9:00 a.m. I opened the garage door and had at least 15 people eager to come into to buy my JUNK! My garage was filled with people when I heard my answering machine answer and a EXTREMELY urgent voice leaving me a VERY irate message.

What happened? I had forgotten that I had booked a Home Party that very morning! Good Grief! ***What would you have done?*** I raced into the house, grabbed the phone and apologized to the Host. She didn't care, she had 15 of her friends there, and they had already had refreshments and where the !@#$%^& was I? She had worked so hard to get everyone there and could I come right away? ***What would you have done?*** I raced to the garage and announced: *"My sale is over for today, everyone, take what's in your hand as a gift from me,*

I am so sorry, but I am now closing my sale, please leave now!" Fortunately, there were only about 10 people there so I didn't lose too much. I raced the crates of products out to my car, threw them in the car, grabbed a lipstick, a skirt and perfume! I jumped in the car, barely had any gasoline in the tank and I hoped I would not run out of gas. I proceeded to the Host home. I was hot and sweaty and worried. At red lights, I fixed my hair, put on some lipstick and sprayed on some perfume.

What happened next: I got to the Host's home and arrived to a group of *very* angry guests. No excuses. I raced in my products and apologized to faces who looked at me like I had bugs coming out of my ears! They were non-forgiving. Not a good scene!

The Show Must Go On: I went right ahead and gave a *great* presentation and at the end, I said, *"Because I caused you this aggravation today of not knowing if I would show up, please everyone take 30% off your orders as my gift to you and to the Host."* I only sold about $300 but that was another $300 towards my sales goals. I didn't book a Party from that Party nor did I get a recruiting lead.

The lesson: I learned another valuable lesson and never missed a commitment again. I also learned to check my diary/calendar every day and to call the Host the day before and double check that the Party was on.

I am committed to staying committed to my commitments.

From a tiny seed
comes a mighty oak tree.
The seed is inside of you.
Mess up as many
times as it takes to learn.
Do not give in or give up.
Do not be denied.

Who Cares Who Dr. Cheng Chong Is?

Don't drone on and on about the technical part of your products or what Dr. this and Dr. that says about them or that some athlete or big name has endorsed. You must *believe in the product enough to be able to convince a Host to schedule a Home Party.* Sell the benefit of what is in your product or why your product will benefit the prospect, Host or guests. Sell the benefits. You don't have to use a third party. If you are believable, people will buy from you and schedule Parties with you. Be credible on your own. You do not need some big name to lean on as a crutch. If your product is great, you can sell it just fine without a big name attached to it. *You are the ticket.*

My Most Fun Party

Story Time: A friend of mine had an idea. Why didn't we get the name and addresses of all the parent's of children in the private schools in North Dallas, Texas and have a fundraiser for the abused children of Dallas? The Party would be held in a HUGE swanky home. We would send out beautiful printed invitations, and have a phone calling committee to call everyone to remind them of the Party. The FREE products would go to the abused children and I would donate a percentage of my commission to the cause. We decided to try it. I contacted everyone I could think of to find someone who had a huge home. I had a nice, comfortable home, but we wanted a showcase home. A successful real estate baron in Dallas came to my mind. I picked up the phone and called his secretary. I told her what I was attempting to do and asked her if he had any clients or associates who might be kind enough to open their home for a fundraiser? She called me right back. The man's daughter had just called and she had shared my idea with her. She was very interested in doing this Party and she gave me her phone number. I contacted Barbara and found out that she had a mansion on Turtle Creek. She loved to entertain and in fact, would send out her own invitation list to 200 people! A bakery supplied FREE pastries in the morning. We had another Party in the afternoon. A steady stream of people came and went both in the morning and the afternoon. The Party was over at 6 p.m. and the phone rang. A complete stranger to me asked me if I could stop by their office on the way home, that they had a check for me to put toward the total amount for the Party. I stopped by that office and picked up the check. The Party was $5,000 and the check was for $2,000. I sold $7,000 that day! Nine people joined to sell the products and I got a lot of FREE products for abused children, plus I donated my *entire* commission. I called the Child Abuse Center, spoke to the Director and surprised them with the toys. From THAT connection, I was invited to set up my products all over downtown Dallas in office buildings in lobbies. In some of those buildings are 5,000 employees, like small towns, and they bought thousands of dollars in product from me for years. From that one idea, grew a huge part of my future business.

Co-Hosting Parties For Others In Party Plan

I have watched for years different distributors try to Host Parties together. I have never seen it work well for any distributor.

Here is why: The other distributors are hoping that you will bring them customers. They will not work hard to provide a group of people for you to prospect and sell to as well. It hasn't worked in my experience. I have found it a waste of time.

Sound Coaching Advice

Dedication of your efforts to the Host may seem unusual at first. But it's not. You will be following the *soundest* of all sales principles, *to think habitually of how you can best serve the interests of your customers.* This may involve relearning past habits until it becomes your habitual method of operation but if you try it you will find that it pays off with a vengeance.

Important: When you look at things like your Host does you will end up selling and recruiting more than you ever dreamed possible.

Result: This approach not only changes what takes place within you (how it dramatically releases your own personal power), but equally important an incredible change will take place in other people's attitude toward you.

Preparation Is Everything

Much preparation goes into having a successful Party. There is much planning behind the scenes. You must be ready. It's like a wedding, building a house, or other special event. So much preparation goes into making sure the foundation is right before beginning to build. Be prepared.

The Host Benefits

The Host has given up their time and house to accommodate your Party, they invited some guests for you, and deserve a reward for their efforts. Such a reward is needed to entice others to hold future Parties. Decide what rewards are suitable, however, the retail profit value from a Party Plan enables the distributor to offer some reward based upon sales made during the event.

Here are the benefits for the Host:

1. **It's a** nice way to get people together.
2. **It's a** fun way to entertain.
3. **You find** that hosting a Home Party is FUN.
4. **You get** a chance to entertain.
5. **You get** a distributor who can give you long-term customer service.
6. **You get** a reason to show off a new or remodeled house to your friends.
7. **You get** free products and/or products at a discount.
8. **You get** to do your friends a service by offering them an alternative to shopping at the mall.
9. **You get** to earn FREE products.
10. **You get** to enjoy shopping and social time with friends.
11. **You get** to hold a great baby shower.
12. **You get** to help children/or their classrooms benefit instead of other businesses.
13. **You get** to make a difference.
14. **You can** give the Host's rewards to charity.

Use the words

YOU GET!

Host Coaching Tips

1: Find out what your Host wants: Talk with them, and let them talk and listen. If you listen, you will get to know what is on their mind and then you can give them, not only kindly, but intelligent help.

2: Schedule the Party with the intention of helping others: Go to the Party, not just to sell something, but with an idea that it will be of some use to the guests.

3: Keep an idea book: This can be done in a spiral notebook or online. Keep notes on what you have found out about their challenges, goals and interests. Make a page or file for each guest. Write down ideas for helping them as they come to you. Take notes on what they tell you.

Example: You might see something online that you can forward to the guests or Hosts because you care.

4: Spend time planning *who* you are going to call: Make calls to prospective Hosts. Set a goal to call more prospects in one day than most distributors do in a week.

5: Take a genuine interest in the personal challenges of others: They will refer business to you. Satisfied Hosts will recommend you far and wide to everyone they know.

Words you want to hear:

"I want to do what you are doing!"

Stay In Touch With Host

Once the Party's scheduled, *it's imperative* to stay in touch with the upcoming Host. Follow up for appointments. Mentally *"make each call"* by rehearsing what you will say on the call. Focus on who you are speaking with. Contact the Host frequently. Leave messages on their answering machine...**Say:** *"I am looking forward to holding your Party and **you get** (Host plan) as a gift! Remember, the more people you have at the Party, the higher the sales, the more (Host plan) **you get**! You get the people there, I will do the rest."*

Get a commitment: Ask the Host if they will *commit* to holding this Party for you? Be clear that *they are clear that they are committing* holding this Party.

Why: You cannot afford to get cancellations. Getting a firm commitment from the Host helps you from getting cancellations.

Say to the Host: *"You get the people there, I will do the rest. We are partners in this. The more I sell, the more **you get**. You can count on me to give THE BEST home Party you have ever been to and you will want to do another one with me!"*

no action=no results

small actions=small results

medium actions=medium results

massive actions=massive results

The Host Pre-Party Calling System

Make a guest list. Call the guests 30 days prior to the Party, 2 weeks prior to the Party to remind them about the upcoming Party, one week prior to the Party and the day before the Party.

Why? Because today, people are very busy and forget or get dates mixed up. It only takes a few minutes and this part of the preparation can pay off greatly for both you and your Host.

Important: Set up expectations with your Host from the very beginning.

Here is how: When scheduling the Party, make sure that you let your Host know that you are partners in making the Party successful.

Important: In Party Plan, *you must* sweat the small stuff!

Written Invitations: You can send postcards or elegant invitations. Or you can simply call people and invite them to come. If you send invitations, ask for an R.S.V.P. Today, many people don't R.S.V.P., that art of politeness is gone from our culture. So, it's best to follow up with a phone call. Invite everyone to bring at least one guest.

We are continuing to prepare for the Party... mental preparation is needed to make it to the top.

Enjoy Working With The Host

If you enjoy working with the Host, you will enjoy what you are doing and you will be successful. Success in any occupation depends upon enjoyment. Loving your work makes the difference. Give your supreme effort every time you do a Party. Bring every particle of your energy, unrelenting resolution, your best efforts, and your best presentation to every Party. Have fun and build a business at the same time or the best will not come out of you. Back up your ambition by your unbounded enthusiasm and determination to be the best which knows no failure. With a massive will, supreme effort, intense and persistent application, you can become one of the top distributors in Party Plan. Have an intense desire to enjoy working with your Host. If the Host sees you having fun, they will tell everyone they know and will be walking Ambassadors for you.

"I rather be a failure in something that I love than a success in something that I don't."
-George Burns

"You will never succeed while smarting under the drudgery of your occupation, if you are constantly haunted with the idea that you could succeed better in something else."
-Orison Swett Marden

"The fact remains that the overwhelming majority of people who have become wealthy have become so thanks to work they found profoundly absorbing...The long-term study of people who eventually became wealthy clearly reveals that their 'luck' arose from the accidental dedication they had to an area they enjoyed."
-Srully Blotnick

Important: Make sure that you set up the expectations **BEFORE** the Party so the Host is prepared for what you are going to do. Make your own script, borrow mine to help get you started.

Set the expectation up front: *"I am looking forward to you being a Host for OUR upcoming Party. I am counting on you to get the people there. I have a few housekeeping items to go over with you... is this a good time?"*

Help The Host With Words To Say

If you give your Host excellent coaching, and take a personal interest in them getting (Host plan), they will know they can't fail working with you. They are likely to schedule Parties over and over again. Here is a sample script. Make your own. You can use mine to help you get started. Don't assume the Host knows what to say.

Get all the expectations clear prior to the Party. No surprises for the Host. This builds trust.

Write your own key words here to say for your own script:

here is a sample script to use......

Host Coaching Script

"For you to get the maximum in FREE products or the most discount on the products you would like to own, I want you to know that we must be partners-for-the-Party for this to happen. Here is what I have found is the best way for this to happen. ***You get the people there, I will do the rest.*** *The more people you get to your Party, the higher the sales, the more (Host plan) you get. It doesn't matter what people wear to the Party. You don't have to have a place for everyone to sit. Here is what I need, either a coffee table, kitchen table or space to show the products. We also need a clean bathroom and for your children to be looked after during the Party. You do not have to do an elaborate dessert because so many people today just want to shop and go. You might want to have water, sodas, beer or wine depending on your guest list. I will arrive about 15-20 minutes early to help you greet your guests and to set up my products which takes only about 5 minutes. I will not pressure your guests to buy but I will be showing them so many items that they will want them all. I am very excited about my business and it's people like you who make it possible for me to not have to have a traditional job (or stay home with my children). My job at your Party is to sell as much as I can, schedule more Parties from the Party and get you the maximum amount of (your Host plan). If I book more Parties from your Party, you get (Host gift). If I recruit people at your Party, you may buy my products from me the rest of your life at 15% off. My presentation lasts only 20-30 minutes. I will be asking everyone to put on a name tag and will be greeting your guests at the front door with you. I will be asking everyone to fill in an order form. I will be doing an icebreaker or game for the first few minutes that will show others how fun it is to have a Party. I will be staying for 30 minutes after the presentation to take orders and answer questions. I will take all of the orders and the money at the Party. I accept all major credit cards and cash.* (Depending on how your company delivers the product make this clear during the Party. Depending on how your company collects taxes on products make this clear during the Party.) *If there are any challenges with products after the customers get their products, I will be in charge of sorting that out for them. Remember, you get the people there, I will do the rest. It's going to be a great Party. I am looking forward to working with you. You can count on me to show up and give you and your guests an outstanding presentation.*

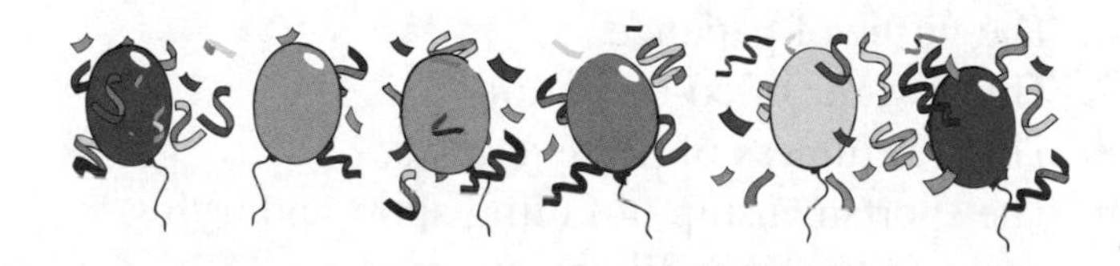

Sample Script For Host Inviting Guests To Their Home Party

"Hi, this is (Host name). I am hosting a Home Party next month for (what company). We are going to have a great time. It's at 7:00 p.m. on Thursday, March 7 and I would love for you to come. The distributor will bring the products, do a short presentation and we can all shop. I have been asked to tell you that they take payment at the Party and they take all major credit cards (adjust this to how your company requires payment). *Come in comfortable clothes, you don't have to get all dressed up. Please bring a friend, the more the merrier! Can I count on you to be there?"* Stop, listen, let them answer.

Next: If the potential guest says: *"Sure, sounds like fun!"* then say, *"Great! Looking forward to seeing you."* If the potential guest says: *"I can't make it, sorry."* (For any reason: out of town, not interested, hates Parties, etc.) Then say, *"I'll get you a catalog and you can place your order prior to the Party so it will still count toward the order. You will love these products and I know you will find several items that you want to own. I'll pop by and leave you a catalog in the next few days and then come back and pick it up with your orders. We will miss you at the Party, it's really going to be fun."*

Make sure your Host gives out pertinent information about the Party.

Don't assume the Host knows what to say. Coach your Host.

Foundation For Success

In building a firm foundation with your Host, here are a few building blocks to remember:

1. The wisdom of preparation.
2. The value of confidence.
3. The worth of honesty.
4. The privilege of working.
5. The discipline of struggle.
6. The magnetism of character.
7. The radiance of health.
8. The forcefulness of simplicity.
9. The gentleness of courtesy.
10. The attractiveness of modesty.
11. The inspiration of cleanliness.
12. The satisfaction of service.
13. The power of suggestion.
14. The buoyancy of enthusiasm.
15. The advantage of initiative.
16. The virtue of patience.
17. The rewards of co-operation.
18. The fruitfulness of perseverance.
19. The sportsmanship of falling short and trying again and again until you succeed.
20. The joy of having a successful Party.

Section 5

Recruiting Your Way To Riches....

Start Spreading The News

You cannot get to the top of Network Marketing holding Parties by yourself. You cannot get to the top alone. To succeed in getting to the top you must recruit and train others to do the same.

Get Trained *How To* Recruit By Someone Who Knows *How To* Recruit

Sit at the feet of the distributor in your company who is recruiting. Do not criticize, be jealous of them or judge them. Learn from them. Use their words, their motions, and their enthusiasm. Copy what works. The sincerest form of flattery that anyone can give you is to copy you.

Train Distributors From The Beginning What Business They Are In

Have you heard: *"I just want to sell, I don't want to recruit." or "I am not ready to recruit." or "I don't know anyone that would want to do this." or "I would like to just get the kit and buy from myself at a discount." or "I don't want to be pushy."*

This is a business where the goal is to **sell, recruit, schedule** and **hold Parties.** The sellers only stick around after a few years even if they have recruited a few people. If you are great at presenting, you almost can't help but recruit. Train those who you recruit to **sell** and **recruit**!

Declare yourself to be a "*Recruiting Professional*"

The Grand Staircase

Visualize a grand entryway staircase. The goal is to get to the top of the stairway. I don't know where you are on your staircase. Each step on that staircase that you step up onto is getting you closer and closer to the top. The idea is not to stop on your way, keep pressing on step by step. Each new distributor that you recruit and train has their own staircase. As you help them to make their goals a reality, you will get to the top of your own staircase quicker.

Let Them Go And Grow

One of the greatest parts of Network Marketing is that you do no have a boss. You are an independent contractor or sales person. You do not have to follow only one proven system and feel like a failure if someone else's system doesn't work for you. I would have never become the top earner in my company all these years if I had followed other's systems. I tried *everything*. If you have a system that gets results, share it with your distributors. As your business grows, not everyone will want to follow your system and you have to let people be creative. Give them roots and give them wings. Distributors will want to start their own meetings, their own teams and their own path. The Upline has no right to demand anything from their distributors. If a distributor in your successline finds a different system than yours and gets results, my advice is to cheer them on and go to the bank.

Show And Tell

The more you show and the more you know and the more you can share about your growing business, the more people you will recruit. Show and tell and show and tell and show and tell, for years.

16 Powerful Ways To Massively Increase Your Recruiting At The Party

Once you realize that you can't possibly get to everyone in your own COUNTRY by yourself and that the money is in recruiting others, you will learn how to recruit others easily at the Parties.

1: The *major* way to recruit at your Parties: Make the guests want so many of your products that they start thinking: *"I can't possibly afford everything I want, I need to either:*

1. *have my own Party or*
2. *become a distributor!"*

How: Practice, drill and rehearse (PDR) your presentation over and over again. Get good at presenting your products and opportunity and you will get rich in Party Plan.

2: Talk about the benefits for the guest to become distributors: Talk benefits, benefits, benefits, benefits, benefits, benefits.

3: Ask for referrals: Often the best distributors come from a friend who knows that their friend would be perfect. We are in the referral business.

4: Ask: Ask people to become distributors and keep asking for referrals.

How: Say: *"Who do you know that might be interested in earning some extra money from home working part-time in the fastest growing business in our area?"*

5: Use Posters: Put posters in various stores and include a sign up sheet for people interested in becoming a Host or attending a Party. It may even be possible to hold the Party at the store.

6: Use Canisters to capture leads: (see page 63)

7: Set up products at a fair and have a *"hands on"* experience for prospects to use the products: Only have a few products available at a time for this. For people to see the whole line, schedule a Party.

8: Create a recruiting flyer to pass out at your Parties: (company name) has opportunities for those people who want to combine an interest in family with a desire to have a supplementary income. The work is fun, hours are flexible, and the money is good. You will be joining a great team with the best training available. Inquire about being a distributor and join today!

9: Be duplicatable: NDAOPCC (**N**ever **D**o **A**nything **O**ther **P**eople **C**an't **C**opy.) Don't be perfect. If you mess up, it's OK. Do the best you can. The idea is to have guests say after watching *your* Party: *"I can do what you are doing and I can do it better!"*

10:Offer the opportunity: What if you don't ask all your guests and someone else DOES? Happens every day. Ask everyone.

11:Don't prejudge: Talk about your opportunity like it is *urgent* that your Host, guests, or someone they know, join you. This is NOT pushy; this is business. Doctors tell you to come back, Dentists tell you to come back, and airlines put pressure on you to make the reservation by a certain time. Come on, get aggressive!

12:Be a Master Prospector: Think of the word STEAM. Who do you know in **S**ales, **T**eachers, **E**nthusiastic people, those with great **A**ttitudes and who needs extra **M**oney? Why your products and your opportunity? Sell yourself and the benefits of your opportunity! Always STEAM.

13: Have Stop & Think brochures and give one to each guest. **Stop and Think** about joining (company). Here's why: (list benefits)

14: Triple your enthusiasm: Make the Party fun so that people want to OWN your products and do future business with you. Smile! Have fun! If you don't enjoy your *work,* why would anyone want to join you?

15: Decide to burn all bridges behind you so that you have no place to retreat: Decide to go for greatness and to quit living a mediocre lifestyle. Be willing and eager to begin a new path in life.

Declare: *"I am a recruiting professional for (company name). My company has given me the responsibility to recruit 5 key people this month. Now that you have seen how easy and uncomplicated having a Party is, perhaps you might be one of the 5 people I am searching for to do the same? Please see me after the presentation so I can get you happily involved."*

16. At Parties have clip boards with a piece of paper labeled *"Future Hosts"*: Interested people can sign up for future dates, pass the clipboard around at every Party.

Here Is Why Recruiting Works...Do The Math

5x5=25

25x5=125

125x5=625

625x5=3,125

Contact People You Pay To Take Care Of You

Contact every person you do business with, everyone. Ask if they are interested in hearing about your business. If not, ask for referrals. Contact Doctors, Dentists, Hair Stylists, Dry Cleaners, etc. Don't be afraid if they reject you, learn to embrace rejection. **Say:** *"I am starting a home based business in this area and wondered if you would be kind enough to give me the names of 3-5 people who you think might like to have a look at it. So, who do you know who might like to explore this?"*

Here is what will happen:

1: They will know someone and give you a lead.

2: They will not want to give you any leads.

Here's what to do if you are given a lead: Follow up on the lead immediately! Leads go cold after 48 hours.

Here is what to do if they don't give you any leads: Say: *"Just to thank you for at least thinking of someone, may I give you a complimentary catalog?"* and say to yourself, *"Oh well, next..."* And then...continue sorting through the public for potential Hosts and recruits.

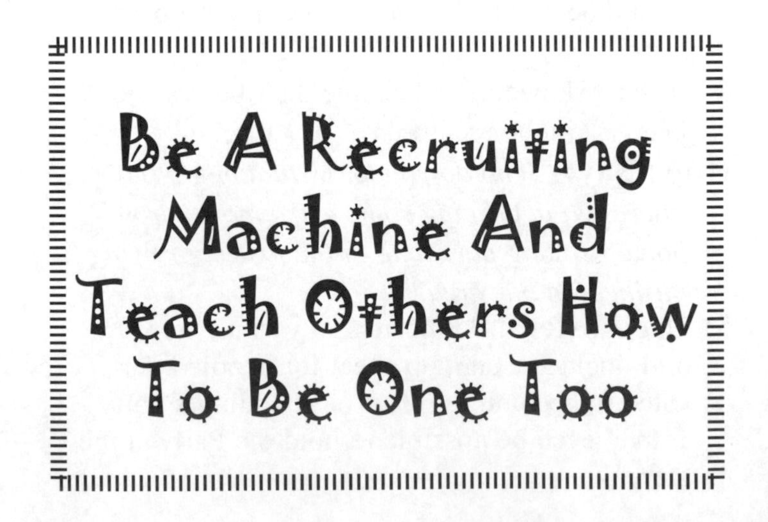

Steps To Recruiting Excellence At Parties

1: Say these words at your Party: *"As I look around the room, I want you all to join me and become distributors right now at the Party. It's so easy to get involved and you can join tonight. If you have 4 or more items you want, it's worth it to have a look at becoming a distributor."*

2: Help people understand the reason you are recruiting: Sometimes they don't understand. Guests need to know that the demand, the need, and interest in what you offer requires many more people than are involved at this time. There are potential customers as well as potential recruits who will never be talked to, who will never hear what you have to offer. There are not enough people to give proper customer service to all available prospects. Recruit consistently, not just on a part-time basis. The rule is to take advantage of every chance you get to share your opportunity. That is what recruiting is all about.

3: Recruiting is helping: There are people who are sad, bored, lonely, broke, broken hearted, unappreciated and who see no future in their company. They can't imagine when they will get a raise in pay and when they get it will be so disappointing that they won't even believe it. There are people totally annoyed with their boss, the boss is probably miserable as well, there are people who want to be their own boss and have no idea of how to make this dream come true. That is *EXACTLY* what you can do. Part time or full time, you can offer hope and a way out. You can help people begin building their own businesses happily in charge of flexible hours, and size of income. The help you offer has lifetime rewards. Give others hope.

Present Your Products/ Opportunity To 500 Or More People A YEAR

Did you know that it's not easy to present your products to 500 people a year? You must present your opportunity to many people to get Party Plan off the ground. You must. It's a numbers game.

Do the math: To present your products and opportunity to 500 people in 365 days, *you must* talk to 44.6 people a month, 11.15 people a week, or 1.3 people a day.

Idea: If you have 52 Parties, one a week and work with the Host to have 10 guests or more attend for an average Party, you have shared your product and opportunity with over 500 people.

The Value Of Recruiting

If you have just one other person doing the same, the 2 of you are reaching 1,000 people a year. It's much easier than trying to talk to 1,000 people by yourself. It's almost impossible to talk to 1,000 people a year. What if you have 100 people doing the same? It's called word of mouth selling or Network Marketing and it leads to wealth.

Do this: Share the opportunity enough and it has to work. It has to start spreading like wildfire. If your presentations are fun and lively, and guests get a "*feeling*" that you are in your company to stay, they will schedule Parties with you.

Party Plan is the Greatest Game in Town

☆☆☆☆☆☆☆☆☆☆☆☆☆☆

Put These On Large Signs Or Banners With Your Display That Says

"Distributors needed, join today! Ask how?"

or

"Thinking about Part-time work from home?"

or

"Want (Host plan)!" Schedule a Party!"

Holding First Parties For New Distributors

I do not believe that Parties where the distributor Hosts the first Party and GIVES the new distributor the total proceeds and all future Parties to that distributor is the correct or smart way to build a business. If you have 10 new distributors, are you available to go out 10 times during the month to get them each started in their business and not use those times to work your own business? What if they all have Parties at the same time? Why not teach them from the beginning that it is simple to do their own Party? Let them come and watch you. Although some people believe this is the way, they don't have any time freedom. They are always so busy being the trainer. Start your new distributors out expecting them to attend a training or take them with you to observe you at the Party. Show them *"how to"* do a Party and let them start from the beginning doing their own Parties.

ATTACH MORE FEAR TO NOT RECRUITING THAN TO RECRUITING.

•••••••••••••

The Fear Of Recruiting

So many distributors think they are being pushy when they ask people to join them. This is rubbish. The only way to survive and thrive in this business, is to have thousands of people each doing a little bit of sales daily. This is the beauty of this business. It's fun. If you fear recruiting then you have your fear attached to the wrong thing. Fear NOT recruiting. Start by saying...*"If I could show you a way...to get out of debt, stay home with your children, to make some additional money...."* Recruiting is fun and it's easy. It becomes a way of life.

SW..SW..SW...Next SW

This will help you when you are discouraged. Keep sorting through the public to find business.

Some will Host a Party with you, buy from you, recruit with you, **some won't, so what, NEXT... someone is waiting.**

When you can't think of anyone else go out on your front walkway and scream

Section 6

Sales.... The Smart Way....

Carry In An Idea Carry Out An Order

Every time you have a Party, carry in an idea for the guests' benefit. This improves your chances of walking out with orders.

Reason: Parties thrive on ideas. Guests welcome ideas and whenever a distributor shares ideas that the customers can use, the customer listens, confidence breeds and the distributor gets business and more business.

Improve Your Skills

Many people look at Party Plan like teaching, acting, speaking, or as something they *"could never do."* Perhaps they can't do it as well as the top distributors at first, but what they don't understand is what practice, exposure, desire, intent, need, studying, determination and satisfaction contribute to making people more skillful than they ever imagined. There are public speakers and famous stars who panic with fear prior to their performances. They are frightened of not being good enough. So they try harder. To be successful in Party Plan is a matter of realizing that the things you *"could never do"* become things you can do and do well simply because you try to continue to improve. You can do it.

We are in the business of:

Selling products

Selling the opportunity

Selling scheduling Parties

Tap Into These 5 Sources

Unless you manage to tap into one of the following 5 sources, whatever effort you make or whatever plan you may set up is doomed to failure.

1: Schedule greater number of Parties: Plan your time better. Devote more of your time to actual scheduling of Parties.

2: Close a greater percentage of guests at the Party to have a Party or join: Work on closing 3 out of 8 instead of 2 out of 8. Develop your closing skills. Learn closing skills. Study sales.

3: Sell large quantities per Party: Plan each Party and prepare for it in advance. Use a planned presentation instead of a hit or miss sales talk; perfect your presentation.

4: Show a wide range of products: Sell *the full line*, rather than only the *"easy to sell items."* Acquire a thorough knowledge of your products. Present them and earn while you learn about the products. Attend trainings, get on training calls, get online training, and find out what to say to make your customers want your products and opportunity. You must sell the products and the opportunity at every Party.

5: Sell higher priced items: Present and sell your more expensive products. Example: If you have items for $10 and under and others for over $10, just present the over $10 products. This increases sales.

What to do: Examine your Party Plan habits, your sales goals, your selling plan and your selling activities in terms of the 5 sources of increased sales. Not every distributor can use each of these 5 sources, but every distributor can make certain that all of their thinking and effort are along lines that lead directly to one or more of these 5 sources.

S.W.I.S.= Sales While I Sleep

You can build a huge, enormous, mega, massive, brilliant, outstanding, incredible business by just doing Parties. If you believe in your product and your opportunity, then share that enthusiastically with groups of people. The more Parties you do, the more energized you will be to recruit more people so that at the same time you are holding a Party you have a huge group of others doing the same and YOU get a percentage of what is sold at those Parties. It's called S.W.I.S., **S**ales **W**hile **I** **S**leep! You must keep your energy up for years in Party Plan. It is a way of life. Teach others to teach others how to hold Parties and your business will mushroom. Sweet dreams!

Fill A Need, Make A Sale

Concentrate On Presenting Higher-Priced Products

The higher priced products are the most profitable products and they take no more of your selling time and energy than the lower-priced, less profitable ones. Concentrate on those products that yield the maximum profit to you. Selling big ticket products takes some imagination and skill. Always show and talk about your high end products.

Million Dollar Monday

Imagine having 50,000 distributors in your successline all selling products on a Monday night. All together you sell a Million Dollars in products. Do you know that happens? How big are you thinking? Once your brain grasps what is possible, and you go into action, you could be one of the top distributors in your company. Why not go for it?

And... why not now?

Creative Selling

A creative distributor creates business where none existed before. No one has a monopoly on creativity. There is something of that quality in every distributor. In fact, most distributors are much more creative than they think they are. Don't underestimate your creative talents. Just picking up orders is not creative selling. You get that business easily without any special effort.

How To Avoid "*Peak* And *Valley* Selling"

A period of low or perhaps literally no productivity can undermine all but the strongest distributor. When the valleys are hit, morale tends to sag. The distributor begins to wonder whether they have *"lost the magic touch."* They begin to question whether their product line is just not right for them. The money slows down, the combination of financial hardship during the *"slumps"* and low morale may cause distributors to quit or to go to another company or maybe even leave Network Marketing. Don't leave, it's always too soon to quit. Concentrate on scheduling more Parties. Send out another Booking Letter. (see page 61) Get more flyers out, get more canisters out. Plug into someone who is fired up. Over schedule. Never ever give up.

How To Avoid The Valleys

Don't get into the feast or famine mentality. When you find that you have several prospects to Host a Party, concentrate your full attention on them but KEEP prospecting for more. Then you don't have to rush people into making a decision. Keep prospecting. Keep working with at least 20 hot prospects every month.

Use Your Imagination

You alone can supply the vital spark of imagination. It is the key to getting to the top in Party Plan.

1: Constantly borrow ideas from others. Get idea minded and you will find ideas that you can adapt here, there and everywhere. In what you read, observe, hear in conversation, or see in use.

2: Adapt ideas that others have used.

3: Originate your own ideas. Act upon them. The biggest dividend to you from your creative ideas is the self confidence you gain.

4: Be eager to obtain knowledge. Be curious. Be curious forever.

Note: The new ideas you need won't just come along, you have to look for them. The harder you look, the more ideas you will find. **Here is how:**

1: Spend 15 minutes a day looking for ideas: Like guests, ideas come only where and when invited; invite some in to your life daily.

2: Read more: Non-readers start far behind the line in getting ideas. Readers are leaders and leaders are readers. The best way is to force yourself to read for a certain period of time every day, whether you like it or not.

3: Learn by talking to other distributors: Even though you might sell something entirely different, interchange ideas in our Network Marketing industry and the sales industry and you will get a transfusion of workable ideas.

4: Travel more: When you travel you learn new things, and you are forced out of your non-thinking rut. You will also meet more prospects.

5: Cultivate older people and listen to them: Senior citizens are wise in the ways of the world and delightful to talk to.

6: Experiment with your own ideas: Be willing to welcome new ideas and be willing to try them out in your Parties.

7: If you see an idea that another distributor is finding profitable, adapt it to your Parties.

8: Consult an expert: Don't be above asking those who are thought to be experts in our industry or in your company to contribute ideas to your success. Whenever you have a chance to talk to or listen to such a person...do it. You will find experts eager to share their knowledge.

Increase Guests' Confidence

Knowledge of your product and your opportunity increases your guests' confidence and raises your own enthusiasm. The distributor who knows their product never has to misrepresent the product they are selling.

1. **Add-on sales:** If you go into a hardware store and buy a flashlight, what are the salespeople trained to ask you? ***"Do you need batteries?"*** That is an example of add-on sales. See where add-on sales could be included in your presentation.
2. **Be knowledgeable of your most expensive products.**
3. **Be proud to be the presenter.**

We've Got a Good Thing Going!

Find Out What People Need And Fill It

Be knowledgeable about your products and opportunity but not a know it all. Be enthusiastic but not giddy. Be cheerful but persistent. Don't talk about yourself. Strangers don't care about you. Talk about the benefits of your products and opportunity to your guests. Sell what's in it for them to buy or to join you. You are there to SELL to the guests there. They have come to BUY your products AND opportunity. If you don't sell the opportunity, you are missing the entire concept of Network Marketing.

Strike At The Guests Needs And The Sale Is Yours

Little sales are often made into big ones if you strike at the customers most important need, and fill it.

Magnify the success of your Hosts. Give recognition to your Hosts

Important Ways To Increase Your Total Volume Of Sales

Give guests at the Party information about your product that will make the guest want to buy. For people to join, you must give them information about the business before you can expect them to join you. Be prepared. Here is how.

Make sure you have enough of your product and opportunity information prior to the Party.

Ask yourself the following questions:

Do I know...

...why the guest is buying our product?
...what the guest is expecting at the Party?
...how the guest is planning to use our product?
...other ways my guest can use our products?
...when the guests expect delivery?
...how to schedule Parties from Parties?
...how to open and close a Party?
...how to make the Parties fun?
...how to recruit at Parties?
...how to sell the benefits of joining our company?
...how to sell the benefits of joining with me?
...how to offer the opportunity in a way that guests want to join at the Party?

Do I have...

...enough brochures
...order forms
...new distributors order forms or whatever forms I need to recruit a lot of people? If a call back is necessary to my Host, have I left my Host with an impression of the product and what's in it for them so that they will want to have a Party? I must remember to sell the benefits to the Host about what's in it for them.

The Modern Buying Approaches Of Guests

Many distributors are not aware of the tremendous changes in buying from distributors in the past 5-10 years. Guests don't buy like they used to. Today's distributor does their best to upgrade their knowledge of the products and techniques, by learning closing techniques that get the guests to want to buy. Buyers want to know W.I.I.F.M., **W**HAT'S **I**N **I**T **F**OR **M**E? Make your presentation about what benefit they will get from owning your products and or joining your successline.

Use Modern Presentation Methods

Buying has become almost a profession. Buyers look to the distributor to aid them in this task. To do this properly, the distributor must be equipped with facts, statistics, data and knowledge of various sorts that would surprise his predecessor of only a decade ago. The demands on the distributor have been accelerated so that today the responsibility as an educator has increased. Parties are the modern way to give a presentation of products and services faster than word of mouth one person to one person. Work on your presentation skills.

SELL The Benefits

The Possibilities Sell The Dream

Don't just sell product only. The idea is to recruit thousands of distributors each doing a little bit. Just think of what your check would look like if you had 25 distributors all out holding Parties, selling the same product as you the same time you are, it's called exponential growth. You cannot force reluctant distributors to sell more. Network Marketing is based on thousands of people moving product. THOUSANDS. All you need is to recruit 5 key people and help them do the same and do that over and over again. That builds a Network Marketing business that does not fail, nor dwindle but instead increases for years.

"We are all ordinary people looking for the opportunity to do extraordinary things."

-Harris Williams

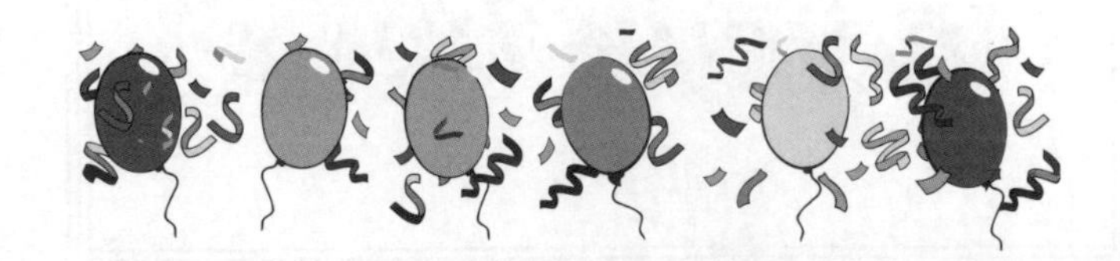

Selling At Home Parties

Parties can make you more money per hour than almost any other form of selling. Parties represent the most enjoyable method of selling. If done correctly, your first Party could be the start of a permanent series, each Party being held by a guest of the previous one. One of the best and least expensive ways to get a quick start in your business is to hold Home Parties. The idea is to make it so simple that anyone can duplicate what you are doing. It's really friends doing business with friends. Party Plan success is all about a lot of people selling a little, as opposed to a few people selling a lot in the conventional companies. Don't have any fear about whether you have enough selling skills when you are getting into Party Plan. You need only sell a small amount as long as you can duplicate your efforts. Think how much bigger your business could be if you were able to sell twice as much and inspire your Successline to do the same.

The More You Know, The More You Sell

The more you know about your products and their benefits, the more you will sell. The best way to learn about your products is to use them and read everything you can about them. Not only do you learn by experience by using your products but you also become more believable in presenting them to everyone who sees you using them. Genuine belief and enthusiasm sell far more effectively than any planned script.

Telling, Not Selling

Talk about your products to everybody; be proud of them, so let everyone know what you sell. Be your own best customer.

People Want You To Tell Them About What You Are Doing

In Party Plan, you have the great advantage of knowing that the people you are looking for are there. The only foolproof way of reaching them is by persisting in showing your business to people Example: If you saw someone drop a diamond worth a million dollars into an huge truck loaded with sand, how long would you spend looking for it? A day? A week? A month? You would spend as long as it takes to find it, because you know it is there. It is impossible not to get where you want to go if you will only keep going.

Sell Desire

In Party Plan, you are looking for a minimum of 5 people like you. People who are looking for more in their life; more money, more time, and more fun. You are surely not conceited enough to think that you are the only person around with such desires? You know there are others like you who can see the attraction of Party Plan who are willing to put some effort into making such a business work for them. They are there, waiting for someone like you to come along and give them an opportunity to change their life to show them how to get what they want. All you have to do it to find them. The difficult part is that the people who want to buy from you and want to join you are very cleverly disguised as normal people. They look exactly like everyone else, with no outward indication that they are the ones you want. You have to talk to them to find out. You have to go through the same procedure with every person, inviting them to be a Host, or to become a distributor, explaining and following up.

Association

Associate with successful people. Avoid people who have a negative and destructive attitude. Seek out people who can uplift and inspire you and help you reach your goals. Don't be too awestruck by someone who earns an income 20 times greater than yours.

"You can't heat an oven with snowballs. One must use firewood of knowledge. Love and belief. You gotta know what's cooking, you gotta love what's cooking, you gotta believe in what's cooking. Success is as simple as that. There is a law of life as strong as the law of gravity. If you want to live a happy, a successful, yes, a fulfilled life, you must LOVE people and use things, not USE people and love things. You gotta BELIEVE in what's cooking. If you really believe in what you are doing, you have everything. If you don't, regardless of what you have, you ain't got nothing."–**Will Rogers**

The Challenge

Let others lead small lives,
but not you.
Let others argue over small things,
but not you.
Let others cry over small hurts,
but not you.
Let others leave their future
in someone else's hands,
but not you.
-Jim Rohn

Buckle Right In

Somebody said that it couldn't be done,
But he with a chuckle replied
That maybe it couldn't, but would be one
who wouldn't say so till he'd tried.
So he buckled right in with the trace of a grin
on his face. If he worried he hid it.
He started to sing as he tackled the thing
That couldn't be done, and he did it.
Somebody scoffed: *"Oh, you'll never do that;*
At least no one ever has done it."
But he took off his coat and he took off his hat,
and the first thing we knew he'd begun it.
With a lift of his chin and a bit of a grin,
without any doubting or quiddit,
He started to sing as he tackled the thing
That couldn't be done, and he did it.
There are thousands to tell you it
cannot be done.
There are thousands to prophesy failure.
There are thousands to point out to you,
one by one,
But just buckle right in with a bit of a grin.
Just take off your coat and go to it;
Just start to sing as you tackle the thing
That cannot be done, and you'll do it.
-Edgar A. Guest

What Is Possible

You can spend every day of the year showing your products and opportunity to people and have 364 refusals (unlikely) but what if the 365th person becomes the most successful distributor in your company? Suppose this happened every year for 6 years. You would have a gigantic business! How many businesses can say that after 6 years? Believe me, it's worth the effort. Success is 1% inspiration and 99% perspiration. The idea is to touch your business every day. There is nothing to lose and everything to gain. Just suppose you could make it work? Isn't it worth a try? No one can start at the top, get started today, stick with it and in 3-5 years, you can have an amazing business. Don't float on the edge waiting for something to happen.

Building A Successful Party Plan Business

What is the definition of *"Success"*? Success is many times equated with financial wealth. Success is defined really as the *"accomplishment of what was aimed at"*. Not everyone in Network Marketing wants a gigantic business, which earns them incredible, outrageous checks, every month and all the hard work that goes into earning them.

2 Important Qualities For Party Plan Success

Party Plan is simple but it is not easy. It is simple because a successful business can be built by repition of an easily learned sales presentation and some genuine enthusiasm about the products and opportunity. It is not easy because the 2 all-important qualities for Party Plan requires success 1) consistency and 2) persistence.

Get What You Want In Party Plan

Most wealthy people will reveal that making a large amount of money was not their prime objective when they got started in Network Marketing. They had a strong desire to do or create something. In striving to reach their goal, they created wealth for themselves. It's not that they made a lot of money, it's that they make a lot of money being successful at what they do. The majority of people in Network Marketing want a reasonable extra income to pay off some of their bills and to treat themselves with a few luxuries now and then. Some are looking to be their own boss for the first time, and of course, handfuls are aiming to be very rich. Party Plan is flexible enough to be able to offer all of these people exactly what they want. You have to decide what you want out of your Party Plan business and begin to work toward it. This book has enough information in it to make you wealthy in Party Plan if you so choose.

Nothing Worthwhile Is Ever Easy

Party Plan is not easy because you will have to overcome a substantial amount of negative reaction, from all kinds of people, even some who are close to you. It's not easy because the growth of your business may not be steady or fast, but it is likely to rise and fall several times before it becomes stable. You will be disappointed by people who you think are going to set the world afire in your business, but do nothing at all with it. There will be times when you think that Party plan doesn't work at all and you might as well quit. Party Plan will work, but only if you work it.

The Essence of Mindless Conformity

One day, through the primeval wood,
a calf walked home, as good calves should;
But made a trail all bent askew,
a crooked trail as all calves do.
Since then 200 years have fled, and
I infer, the calf is dead.
But still he left behind his trail,
and thereby ends my moral tale.
The trail was taken up next day,
by a lone dog that passed that way;
And then a wise bellwether sheep,
pursued the trail o'er vale and steep,
And drew the flock behind him too,
as good bellwethers always do.
And from that day, o're hill and glade,
through those old woods a path was made;
And many men wound in and out, and dodged,
and turned and bent about
And uttered words of righteous
wrath because 'twas such a crooked path.
But still they followed, do not laugh,
the first migrations of that calf,
And though his winding wood-way stalked,
because he wobbled when he walked.
This forest path became a lane,
that bent and turned and turned again;
This crooked lane became a road,
where many a poor horse with his load,
toiled underneath the burning sun,
and traveled some 3 miles in one,
And thus a century and a half,
they trod the footsteps of that calf.

The years passed on in swiftness fleet,
the road became a village street;
And this, before men were aware,
a city's crowded thoroughfare,
And soon the central street was this,
of a renowned metropolis;
And men 2 centuries and a half,
trod in the footsteps of that calf.
Each day a hundred thousand rout
Followed the zigzag calf about;
and o'er this crooked journey went,
the traffic of a continent.
A hundred thousand men were led by
one calf near 3 centuries dead.
They followed still his crooked way,
At least 100 years a day;
For thus such reverence is lent,
to well-established precedent.
A moral lesson this might teach,
were I ordained and called to preach;
'for men are prone to go it blind,
along the calf-paths of the mind,
and work away from sun to sun to
do what other men have done.
They followed in the beaten track,
and out and in and forth and back,
And still their devious course pursue,
to keep the path that others do.
But how the wise old wood-gods laugh,
Who saw that first primeval calf!
Ah! Many things this tale might teach,
But I am not ordained to preach!

-Sam Walter Foss

Section 7

The Actual Party....

The Actual Party

The entire first part of this book is all about preparing yourself and your Host for the Party. Now we get to the actual Party and if you are prepared, you will have a successful Party. If you don't prepare, you could be disappointed. If a sports team is unprepared for the game...it shows. When you are prepared, you get to build a business others can only dream of. Before you depart your car to go into the house, leave your troubles on the trouble tree.

The Trouble Tree

Leave all your troubles on a tree outside your home that you name THE TROUBLE TREE. Don't carry your troubles into the Party. Just leave them on the tree. They will be there when you want them. If you get to a private home and you are still upset, mentally hang your troubles on a tree or bush in their front yard.

Practice, Drill and Rehearse your Presentation

Practice, Drill
Rehearse
Practice, Drill
Rehearse
Practice, Drill and
Rehearse
Practice, Drill

The Magic Words That Will Bring You Riches

Most companies have their own magic words. Get to know the terms used in your business and use them. Pay attention to a few words that will reduce fear in your guests. Change these words and you will get better results.

Don't Use	**Use Magic Words**
contract	***paperwork*** or ***application***
sign	***autograph, or endorse***
buy	***own***
deposit	***initial investment***
total due	***total investment***
join up	***happily involve***
pitch	***presentation***

Use The Cash-Register Word The TV Way

The word that makes cash registers ring is ***"NEW"***. Listen to the TV announcers and note how many times they use the word ***"NEW"***. It's repeated and repeated.

Sentence, Sentence, Sentence

The best presentation is when the distributor says five statements and then asks a question or makes a point. Don't go on, sentence, sentence, sentence. Every five statements, ask a question.

Best days to hold Parties is *EVERY* day!

Timing Of The Party

Parties can be held at any time of the day. When your children are young, you can choose to do Parties 1-2 nights a week minimum. As they get into school, you can choose to hold Parties during the day and schedule weekend Parties. The idea about Parties is to work them around your family or your schedule. Let people know when you are available and most will adjust to your schedule.

Do this: *Be dependable*. Never cancel once you have the Party scheduled. Get the reputation that you are *dependable*. Decide with your Host what time you wish to hold the Party.

When to start the Party: Always start no later than 15 minutes after you say you are going to start. Do not penalize the people who get there on time for those who don't respect invitational times. You can explain to those late comers what they missed later.

AIM, GET READY, GET SET, FIRE UP! GET READY... THE PARTY IS ABOUT TO BEGIN

The Party Pre-Flight Check Off List

Just as a pilot goes through his checklist before taking off the runway, so should Party Plan distributors. Use a check list for your first 20 Parties.

1. **All stickers off your car:** Only stickers selling your opportunity.
2. **Arrive at the Party and say to yourself:** *"I am going to give my most important presentation of my career. I am at the top of my company. This is going to be fun!"*
3. **Arrive sober** with no smell of alcohol.
4. **Be smart and clean.**
5. **Clean vehicle.**
6. **No smoking.** Those who are non-smokers will not schedule a Party with you.
7. **Don't dress up.** No dirty denim.
8. **Don't run out of Gasoline.**
9. **Floss teeth.**
10. **Get nails fixed.**
11. **Have a manicure,** no dirty fingernails.
12. **Have an up-to-date hair cut.**
13. **Have up-to-date glasses.**
14. **Have umbrella in car.**
15. **Have clean samples.**
16. **Have inventory to sell at the Party.**
17. **Have order forms ready.**
18. **Practice your presentation.**

Present To All Personalities

Make SURE to present to the ***guest's*** personality. Not yours. Guests don't want to hear YOUR reasons for doing what you are doing. They are interested in how *THEY* can benefit from what you are saying.

Here is how: Pass products around, let the guests touch and look at them, make sure the price description is on them. Smile, look happy. Make your words paint the picture of how the guests can see themselves joining you.

Arrival

Arrive about 15-20 minutes early as promised. Set up trust and dependability so that your Host will want to re-schedule a future Party with you. Do not park right in front of the house, park across the street so that guests can park closer to the house.

You Are At The Front Door

Go to the front door of where the Party is to be held. Do not take any products with you at first. Ring the doorbell or knock on the door and have a nice smile on your face when the Host opens the door. If you have not met face to face yet, this is their first impression of you. Go into the house and after your initial greeting with the Host say these words: *"Where would you like me to place the products?"* The Host will guide you to where they have chosen the best location in their home.

Then say: *"For the next few minutes, I will be bringing my products in and look forward to meeting your guests with you at the front door in a few minutes. My set up just takes a few of minutes, it's very easy. You can start shopping as soon as I bring the products in. I'll be right back."*

Now what? You need ...

...your products!

Get products out of your vehicle now.

Getting The Products Into The Location Of The Party

Depart the house, go to your vehicle and get your products. Don't try to bring in too much at a time. You will be showing your Host that it is hard to carry in so many products. Even if it takes you 3-4 trips to your vehicle to get products, make the trips. Your Host could be watching you to see if they want to do what you are doing. Once you have the products in the house, set the up as quickly as possible. No need to be fussy or acting like the set up is to be perfect. Just get the products in the house, set up and be ready to Party!

Next: Have order forms ready; your calculator where you know where it is, if you need one; your business cards, marker and straight pins ready and by the front door. Ask your Host if there is anything you can do to help them in those last few minutes to get ready for the Party.

Note: Sometimes the Host is scared to death that you are going to pressure their guests. It's the distributors job to reduce fear. Here is what to ...

Say: *"I am looking forward to your Party and to relieve you, I am not going to pressure your guests to buy or to join me. I am here to get you (Host plan) and to have a great time. We get new products in every month), before everyone gets here, would you like to schedule another Party with me? I will get my (calendar) and after the Party pick a date. Tell me about your guests"*...and off you go. The Host will start talking until the guests start arriving.

The Guests Begin To Arrive

Now it's time to go into action. You have prepared for this moment and now is the time for you to strut your stuff. It helps to wear a name badge to let people know you are the distributor giving the Party.

Guests Are Coming To Shop And To Buy

Most guests come in with a set amount they are willing to spend. Give them a great presentation and you will be amazed at what people spend at Parties. You are the ticket.

Meet The Guests At The Front Door

Shake guests' hands as they arrive and introduce yourself. Look your guests in the eye and **Say:** *"Hi, I am the distributor for tonight's presentation. I am so glad you came. We will be starting the presentation very soon. While we are waiting, tell me your name and how you are connected to the Host."* Listen for what is of **value** to your guests. You will learn a lot about them in a few minutes that you can then use in your presentation. Take notes if you have to.

Come From Contribution

Think of how you can contribute to the happiness of the guest. A happy guest always returns.

When To Begin The Actual Presentation

At the time the Party is to begin, ask the Host if they would like you to wait a few more minutes for the latecomers but no more than 15 minutes before you start. Don't penalize those who come early to wait on those who are late.

A.B.S.= Always Be Selling

A.B.R.= Always Be Recruiting

You are prepared. You have coached your Host.
You have learned the benefits of your products and offering the opportunity.
You have practiced your scripts and are ready to go to the Party...

Good Luck and Have Fun!

Your guests are coming to see what this is all about...give them a fabulous presentation and a fun memory!

IT'S SHOW TIME

Let's Party!

Let's Party!

Let's Party!

Let's Party!

The Party Begins

You are in charge of starting the Party. It's your turn to shine. **Say:** *"May I have your attention? Let's go on and start the presentation."*

The First 10 Words

Your first TEN words out of your mouth are the most important of the Party. Practice, drill and rehearse them. Remember to use the *magic* words. (See page 104)

Name Tags

Direct guests first to your business cards, have them print their first name only, LARGE so others can see it and pin it on their coat or blouse or shirt. They will LEAVE with your business card pinned on them. You can be sure that they will have it when they leave the Party.

Immediately Direct Guests To Your Products

Suggest guests make a wish list of everyone they need a present for coming up in the next couple of months. This may or may not work for your product. Do this if it applies.

Always Ask For More Parties

During your presentation ask for future Parties. We call those *"Booking Seeds."* Plant the seeds for future bookings in your opening, during your Party and in your closing. As you take orders, ask *"So would you like to schedule a Party in your home at this time, I have 4 openings left next month?"*

Just SAY IT!

Ask, Ask, Ask

Script For Scheduling Parties From Parties

Say: *"If you wish to Host your own Party and GET (Host plan) please see me after the Party. I have my datebook with me and we can schedule your Party now. I only have 6-8 openings left this month."*

Important: Spend time on scheduling Parties from Parties and recruiting new distributors to join you and get happily involved at the Party if possible.

Work On Getting Future Parties Scheduled At The Actual Party

Make Guests Want Everything

Present your products in a way that everyone wants everything that you present. Get on eye level or below eye level to present your products if you have just a few guests at the Party. With a lot of guests, stand while you present. The idea is to have them think "*I just came tonight to check this out or to have fun or to get some products, help a friend out.*" to... "*Gee, I want all of these products, I should have a Party or become a distributor myself.* " If you can move people's thoughts to Host a Party or to get happily involved in selling your product, you are well on your way to success.

The 12 Point Party Opening

Put these key words on an index card until you memorize them. Here is what to talk about first:

1. **Welcome** everyone.
2. **Say your name.**
3. **Thank the Host.**
4. **Say that you love your product and opportunity** and if anyone is interested in getting happily involved with you in the business that they can see you after the Party is over. (Plant the seed early.)
5. **State time there.** Say you will be presenting your products for only 20 or so minutes and LOOK at your watch. Stay true to your word.
6. **Delivery** of the products. Order forms, whatever your company requires.
7. **Pass out the Application to JOIN first.** One of the main reasons you are there is to recruit others to do the same.
8. **Let guests know that the products are all marked with the price.**
9. **Let guests know** that the products you are showing during the Party might only be available at the time of the Party. Products might not be available at a later date.
10. **Let guests know how they will be paying.** *"We take all major credit cards"* or whatever your company requires.
11. **Explain if there is a tax or shipping charge.**
12. **Explain the order form.**

You are the ticket!

Stand Up When Saying Your Opening Script

Stand up when you say your 12 Point Opening. Your first words: *"Does everyone have a pen?"* (If they don't supply them with a pen). **Next say:** *"I am eager (or whatever your word is) to show you these products that will (share the benefits) or whatever you want to quickly say to describe your product."*

Eye Level Selling

When you start presenting the products, get on eye level or below eye level with your guests. If the guests sit on a couch, you, the distributor sit on the floor to present. Adjust this to your product.

Be The Life Of The Party

Say: *"We are going to play a quick game just to have some fun."* and play a quick game. Keep the games QUICK, fun and easy. Plan to talk about no more than 10 products and then go into your close. The tempo of the Party will go with you, the distributor. If you are having fun, your guests will too.

Training Others To Do Parties During The Party

On the job training. If you have distributors at your Party observing you giving the Party, introduce them. Let guests know that it's easy to join you and get trained, that they can also come along and listen in when they join.

Make everyone want every product

Sample Opening Script

"Hi everyone! Welcome to our Party this evening. My name is (your name). Thank you to (Host) for having us all in your beautiful home. It's been great to work with you to get this Party organized. Thank you (Host)! I will present the products for about 20 minutes to show you how they can benefit you and your family. I know you will want everything you see. I take all major credit cards and request payment tonight. There is no way that I can assure you that the products you see tonight will still be available tomorrow. How many of you have ever been to a Party? As I look around the room I want you to all either get happily involved and do what I am doing, which is working part time showing these fabulous products while raising my family, or schedule a Party with me in your area. I would love to meet your friends and get you (Host plan)! Then we are going to play a quick game and have some fun. I am going to show you a few items. I will stay for 30 minutes to answer your questions and take your orders. I have a calculator with me and I will tally up your order for you. How easy is that? Our company has a small shipping and handling investment and we collect sales tax. Parties are fun! I want you to remember me, (your name) whenever and wherever you are, when you think about getting happily involved in a home based business. I want you to remember me! That's why I asked you to pin my business card on you tonight! All the products are marked with the price on them so you are welcome to have a look when I am through. Then you can decide what you wish to own. Here we go..."

Start presenting your products.

End The Party Like You Are Slamming A Car Door Shut

1. **Thank your Host.**
2. **Remind** guests you will be there for 30 minutes to take their orders, answer questions, schedule more Parties, and to get those who are interested happily involved.
3. **Schedule more Parties.** Have your calendar ready.
4. **Take orders.** Have calculator ready.
5. **Invite** guests to browse product display. Make sure that guests have time to put their hands on the products.
6. **Answer questions** and help guests complete order forms.
7. **Sell the benefits** of joining you or hosting their own Party.
8. **Be the most enthusiastic person there!** When you love what you do, it shows.
9. **Begin to pack up** products 30 minutes after the close. Make this look easy.
10. **Have a secure place** to put the orders, and any money collected.
11. **Place orders immediately.**
12. **Do not hold** your Party order open. This is an insult to the people who came to the Party. Put in an additional order if you have to.
13. **Give more** than the customer expects. Under promise and over deliver.

Sample Closing Script

"Thank you ALL for coming to this fun Party! (Host) out did herself getting you all here, thank you again (Host) and I look forward to scheduling another Party with you soon. Well, that concludes our Party! I will be here for 30 minutes to answer your questions, schedule your Party, to get you happily involved and to say good night. I have the ending to a poem I would like to share with you all. As you can tell I am very passionate and proud of the products that I represent. You are the best teachers your children are going to ever have. Don't leave their education up to someone else. It is my hope that with these products that your children will increase in their discovery and their self esteem will grow and prosper. I thank you from the bottom of my heart for choosing to come tonight, you could have done many other things and yet you chose to come here. I look forward to being your distributor all year long. You have my business card pinned on you so don't forget about me! I am a phone call away all year long. Here is the ending to the poem I so dearly love..."

***"Into my hand he placed the key,
come mommy, come play with me."***

***Now, please have a look and place your orders.
We are done!***

Then let everyone shop, take orders,
and get people happily involved!
It's that easy!
As you take the orders,
ask each person individually
if they would like
to schedule a future Party.

What To Do After The Party

Once you are ready to leave, thank the Host, take your samples to the car and depart. Get on your cell phone and call someone in your successline to tell them all about your Party. Call home and let family or friends know where you are and what time you will arrive home.

The D.A.C. Formula Make "Day After Calls"

Call the Host the following day thanking them for having the Party. **Say:** *"Thank you for hosting the Party last night. I enjoyed meeting you and your friends. Here are the total sales. I am very happy with them. You worked hard and I am so please that you got (Host Plan) Would you like me to save a date for you to do another Party in the future? I am already scheduling for (month)."* Ask if they had a good time, could they make any suggestions for improving your Party or presentation. Call every single guest at the Party and individually thank them for their orders and then ask them who THEY know who might be interested in having a Party with you.

Say: *"Who do YOU know who might be interested in hosting a Party with me."*

Then say: *Thank you again, I will be keeping you informed of new products as they are added to our line. Thank you again. Bye bye.*

Thank You Notes

Put a hand written thank you note in the post or send a thank you email. So few people get thank you notes. Small touches make a gigantic difference in Party Plan.

Create Goodwill And More Referrals

Send Thank You notes. How many purchases did you make last year? How many Thank You notes did you receive? Probably only two or three, if that. It's rare for anyone to show appreciation today. People crave appreciation and recognition. You can give your prospects, Hosts and guests this appreciation and recognition inexpensively with a simple postcard thank-you note that acknowledges their contribution to your success. Customers and prospects will love you for this simple act of courtesy.

Thank Hosts, Guests And Prospects

There are lots of reasons why you should thank your prospects. Don't limit your thank you notes to just Hosts and customers. The goodwill you build can help get you referrals, and your prospects and customers will always feel favorable to you when the time is right for them to buy or join your opportunity. Thank people for:

* Placing an order.
* Bringing a friend to the Party.
* Reviewing your catalog, recruiting brochure, video information pack, etc.
* Coming to last night's Party.
* Trying the samples you sent them.
* Answering your ad.
* Having the courtesy to tell you that your opportunity wasn't for them.

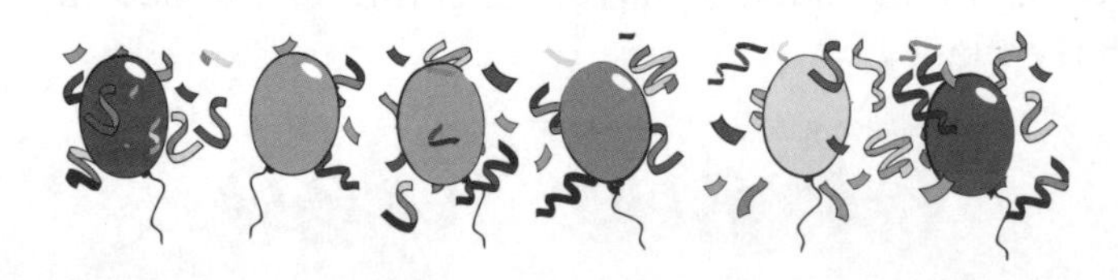

Next... Schedule more Parties and train others to do the same!

Continuously Remind Prospects Of Upcoming Parties

Special guest speaker, (your name) shares
(products)
Saturday
from 7 - 9 p.m.
**All the free food you can eat at Thursday night at David's Annual (product) Party*

* Once-a-year (your product name) sale starts on December 31st.
* Free business start-up kit to the first two who come to my March 1 Party at my home.
* Brand new product introduction.

The 100th Monkey

In his book, The 100th Monkey, by Ken Keyes, he recorded the findings of a scientific study. Thc study was sponsored by the National Geographic Society. They witnessed what is named the Critical Mass Theory. This phenomena is unexplainable by ordinary scientific methods, yet it works throughout life. It is so much like Party Plan and the possibilities for you in your business.

The time frame was 1952 to 1958. The place was a number of Islands in the South Pacific. The explorers were several scientists. The purpose was to observe and record the characteristics and habits of the local plant and animal life. The monkeys who inhabited these Islands were part of the study. The scientists would give them names and record their activities in a journal. The monkey's main food source was sweet potatoes, which the scientists scattered on the ground. The monkeys liked the taste of the raw potatoes, but found the dirt unpleasant.

On the Island of Koshima, a young female monkey named Bilbo found that she could solve the challenge by washing the potatoes in a nearby stream. She taught this by example to her mother and other monkeys, who also taught their mothers. This cultural innovation was gradually picked up by other monkeys. During the six month period many of the Koshima monkeys learned to wash sweet potatoes in order to make them more tasty. But it was only the adult monkeys who imitated their children that learned this improvement in their society. In late 1958, something amazing took place; a new era began. The exact number of monkeys who had learned to wash their sweet potatoes were unknown. But one morning, when that number reached they think 100 monkeys it happened. On one afternoon almost every monkey in the troop was washing its sweet potatoes. Next, the most surprising thing happened. The scientists found that the habit of washing sweet potatoes suddenly and spontaneously jumped over the sea. Colonies of monkeys on other Islands and mainland monkeys, began washing *their* sweet potatoes.

When a certain critical number achieve awareness, this new awareness can be communicated from mind to mind. Although numbers may vary, the 100th monkey idea means that when a limited number of distributors know of a new way, a point is reached where only one more person needs to plug into the new awareness to cause it to reach almost everyone else. You may be the 100th person. You may be the one who finds a way to spread your business to another region or area.

Alternatives

There is no hard and fast rule that Parties must be done in a Home. They can be done in a meeting room, at a luncheon, a park, an office, or any place people congregrate.

How To Approach People

The best advice is to be aware of those around you: See what magazines or newspapers people are carrying. Comment on an article or the headline and then say, *"What do you do?"* If prospects have packages look for the store name and start up a conversation. Hand people your business cards and ask for theirs.

Not Everyone Will Buy Or Join

Not everyone at the Party will buy from you, wants to talk to you, cares that you exist or is interested in your products and opportunity as you are. If you understand this before you go in to your Party, you won't be upset when you are rejected or ignored. Don't take yourself so seriously. Keep telling yourself that you are perfect as your are in that moment and keep working on your sales and presentation skills.

Never Be Late

1. Be early; it's money in the vault.
2. Being late is low priority. Being early is the first step on your financial ladder.
3. Time is money.

Be an inverse paranoid: decide the world is conspiring for you

Attention Grabbers Sell Yourself

- **Name Tags:** On the first line of your name tag, put what you do in big bold letters. Then put your company name or your name. This is a great way to start a conversation.
- **Don't hover:** Guests hate it if you hover.
- **Business Cards:** Have them enlarged and laminated. Wear it attached to a name badge. Conversation starter. Cut up a book cover of your favorite book and have it sized down and laminated and wear that as your name badge.
- **Smile, look interested:** Give off the vibe that you are approachable, and that you have something to offer.
- **Be confident** that what you have to say is interesting and what you have to say will be interesting.
- **Know who is coming to the Party:** Ask for a reservation list before you get there so you can target your guests.
- **Don't sit with friends:** If someone is at the Party you know well, split. You are always at the Party to meet and greet new guests.
- **Reach out:** Always talk to all the guests at the Party.
- **Keep moving, circulate:** After your presentation and taking orders, pack up your products and if you have time, mingle.
- **Be the presenter:** Not the guest.
- **Follow up:** Follow up. Follow up.
- **Make it fun:** Embrace curiosity.

Don't be a collector of your own business cards

Section 8

Games To Play At Home Parties....

Fun Party Games

These are some fun ideas I have tried through the years. Some are seasonal that you can adapt to the current holiday. Having a Party soon? Try some of these, makes life more FUN!

Vegetable or Fruit Game

First: Please separate yourselves into two teams.

Explain the Game: *"I am going to read some fill in the blank statements that have answers that are all fruits or vegetables. The first guest to call out the answer scores a point for their team."*

Hint: (Sometimes you might have to give guests a hint at the first letter). Add your own ideas to the list. Keep game short and quick.

What do they get? Each team member of the winning team that gets the most points, gets $5 off all orders over $30.

1. My Darling **Sweet Potato**.
2. My Heart **Beets** for you.
3. I want a 3 **Carrot** ring.
4. My love for you is as strong as an **Onion**.
5. With your **Radish** hair and your **Turnip** nose.
6. You are the **Apple** of my eye.
7. I know we will make a happy **Pear**.
8. So **Lettuce** start the presentation of (your products)...

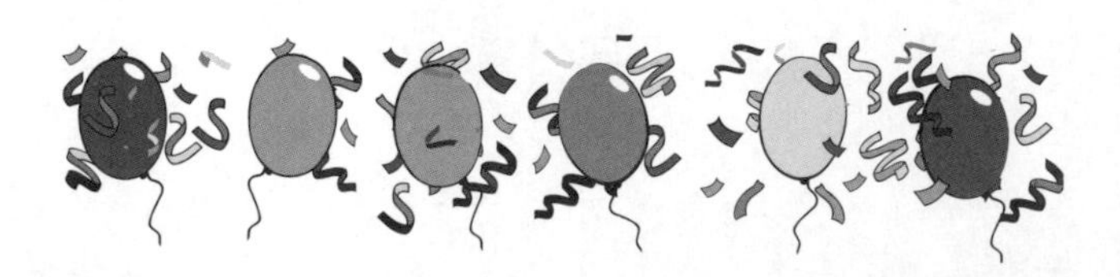

Icebreaker

First: Give each guest a piece of paper and pen.

Explain the Game: *"I am going to ask you some questions and you get to score yourselves."*

What do they get? Prize, product or discount on their order at the Party.

Here is what to say:

I wonder who came here from afar?
Give yourself 5 if you came by car.
Were you on time? Not a minute late?
Punctuality pays so give yourself 8.
A watch is worth 6 and each ring is worth 2.
10 more points if your eyes are blue.
Score yourself 5 if you're wearing any pink.
But take away 10 if you left dishes in the sink.
Count all your buttons…each gives you 1.
Except if they are white and then you get none!
Now for each bow you have on, you may now add 2.
But safety pins are a taboo. So for each you are wearing, you must subtract 2.
Add 1 point for each year you've been wed.
And if you are single we won't debate, we'll assume you're ecstatic so go ahead and add 8.
Now sons are neat, on that we agree, so for each of your sons, add 3.
But when adding up points, girls are worth more, so for each of your daughters, add 4.
If you kissed your husband or boyfriend goodbye, add 12, but into your personal life we must delve…
If you kissed them BOTH you must subtract 20, because you're in trouble and in trouble a plenty!
Now that's all there is, so total your score, except if you are a special friend, then there's one more...
It's a 50 point bonus for a VIP! If you'll Host a Home Party with me!

Old Song Titles Game

Explain the Game: *"See if you can complete the song titles using words connected with love, romance and marriage."*

Hint: Use this list or make up your own songs that your age group knows.

What do they get? Guest who gets them all right gets a discount on their order.

1. **Heartaches** By The Number.
2. Candy **Kisses**.
3. Hawaiian **Wedding** Song.
4. I'll Hold You In My **Heart**.
5. Indian **Love** Call.
6. Your Cheatin' **Heart**.
7. Hunk a Hunk of Burnin **Love**.
8. Get Me To The **Church** On Time.
9. Let Me Call You **Sweetheart**.
10. Cupid, Draw Back Your **Bow**.

Word Game

Explain the Game: *"While we are waiting for everyone to arrive, since you are here early, please take a complimentary catalog and let's play this game. As you look at the catalog to decide what you would like to order today at the Party, in the next three minutes, see how many letters on products can you find that start with letters that spell (your company name)"*

What do they get? Prizes for first, second and third place winners.

The Get New Distributors Game

Prior to the Party: Get a few catalogs. Cut out descriptions from your catalog of your products.

Next: Cut the descriptions into strips so you have one description per strip. Use any special offers you have (i.e., Bonus Buys, Host Only Gifts, free merchandise for holding a Party, recruiting brochure, recruiting information, etc.).

Next: Either have each guest pick one strip from a basket as they enter the Party or place each strip next to the specific item it names.

Explain the Game: *"Please pick a product and description strip. Each guest will have a chance to read the description of how that product could benefit you. It's fun for me to watch the guests present the products to each other. Go ahead and have some fun. All you have to do is to read the product description on your strip of paper. This makes the Party so fun! Thanks for participating."*

Next: After your Opening to the presentation, have each guest *"present"* their item. This is good if you'd rather not demonstrate your products that night or to see which guests in attendance might make good distributors (aren't shy, have a great personality, etc.)

What do they get? Fun! They also get to pay attention to the products more.

It's so easy to spend when you are having fun

The ABC Game #I

Explain the Game: *"Each of you will turn to the person on their left and by using consecutive letter of the alphabet, they say: "I love this product because it is: (example: Attractive, because it doesn't Break, Cost is minimal, etc.)" We will continue until each guest has a turn and you have used the entire alphabet."*

What do they get? Fun!

The ABC Game #2

Explain the Game: *"While we are waiting for everyone to arrive, since you are here early, please take a complimentary catalog and let's play this game. For each letter of the Alphabet, can you name a (put your product name) that starts with that letter that is in our catalog today, or here in my display today?"*

What do they get?

Prizes for the guest who gets the most letters before you start your presentation.

The Tricky Game

Explain the Game: *"Please write the name of 2 friends, 2 relatives, 2 neighbors and 2 other people. Now your guest list is already made out for when they decide to have a Party. Pretty tricky, don't you think?"*

What do they get? The first one finished wins a prize out of your prize basket.

> *"I can't wait to see who wins."*

The Listening Game

Change this game a little if you have repeat guests.

Explain the Game: *"I am going to tell you a little about me briefly and I want you all to listen carefully. At the end of my short talk, I am going to ask you a question to see if how well you listened. Here is a sheet of paper and a pen to take notes."*

Next: Do your short talk while passing out the order forms or catalogs, and casually walk around.

What do they get? Listening skills.

Brief Talk About Yourself:

My name is (your name)

My husband/boyfriend's/girlfriend/partners name:

My children's name:

How long you have been married or single:

How long you have been representing your companies products and opportunities:

How much the $$$ in sales you have done in the past. ($10,000 in one month, etc.)

Incentive trips you have been on.

Next: When you finish with the talk, then **Say:** *"OK... #1 what is my partners name?"* You will get a lot of, *"OH...I wasn't listening."* You can bet that they will listen when you start your presentation.

Next Say: *"Thanks for listening, I want to introduce myself and let you all know that this business is so easy. As I look around the room, I want you all to join me in this business. It's an amazing opportunity. All we do is invest in a kit of products. Our company pays us to set the products up in homes around the country and share them with others. And we get PAID to do this! The products are great and (list some benefits) and if you would like to do what I am doing, please see me after the presentation to join. It's simple to join today or Host your own Party. Schedule it today!"*

Getting To Know You Game

Explain the Game: *"Please take 2 items out of your handbag, pocket, or wallet that best describes who you are."*

Next: Have each guest hold each item up where everyone can see it and explain how it describes who they are.

What do they get? Give a prize to each person that participates.

Benefit: This gives you information on how your company can fit into their life. It is a great way for the guests to get to know about each other.

Example: Take your cell phone out of your handbag or pocket and say something like *"I love to talk on the phone. I get to meet and talk to so many new people, I love my job!"* or tell them you are very sensitive. "*I get teary when I tell my children 'Goodbye' and jet away with my partner for an all expenses paid trip somewhere in the world compliments of my company for just sharing these products! Never in my wildest dreams did I think I would ever travel to (destinations), especially for free!"*

Valentine's Day Week Or Month Theme

Decorate your display table with red hearts and bows. Show off items that go with Valentines Day. Wear something red or pink.

> The road to the top
> is dotted with many
> tempting parking places

Halloween Day Week Or Month Theme

Send invitations to your Party:

On invitations put: *You are invited to a very special (company name) Party with a Halloween theme. To help you enjoy the season and have some Halloween fun ... earn as many game points as you can prior to the Party by doing the following:*

1. Wear something black or orange
2. Bring a colored leaf
3. Bring a friend who places an order
4. Wear a Halloween mask
5. Arrive on time
6. Bring a Jack-O-Lantern
7. R.S.V.P.
8. Bring an outside order from someone else
9. Bring this invitation & brochure
10. Schedule your own (company name) (date)

What do they get? The guest with the most points gets a prize or discount on their order placed at the Party.

The Barnyard Animal Game

Explain the Game: *"Please write down your favorite barnyard animal, as long as it is NOT the rooster, and five numbers between 1-20. I am going to call out numbers, and the guests who have that number have to make the sound of the animal they wrote on their paper. Barnyard animals are not shy, so there should be a lot of loud sounds. Go on and have some fun! The first guest who has all 5 numbers called out that they wrote down, they win...and NOW...then to get your prize, you have to stand up, bend your knees, flap your 'wings' and crow like a rooster. Several can win at the same time!"*

What do they get? Prizes, products or discount on orders placed at the Party.

The Easter Greetings Game

Explain the Game: *"Please write the answers to the following questions. When you are finished, read down the first letter to find an April Greeting from me (Happy Easter)!"*

What do they get? An Easter greeting.

Donald Duck's second Nephew **Hewey**
March Winds bring **April** Showers
Little Jack Horner found it **Plum**
Pig friend of Bugs Bunny **Porky**
He rode to town on a pony **Yankee Doodle**
Winnie the Pooh's Donkey friend **Eeyore**
What fell on Chicken Little's head **Acorn**
What frightened Miss Muffet **Spider**
Bambi's rabbit friend **Thumper**
Bugs Bunny steals carrots from **Elmer Fudd**
Sing a song of six pence a pocket full of **Rye**

The *"Ask Me"* Game

Explain the Game: *"At the end of our Party, we are going to play a quick game. You will get three minutes to ask me ANY question about MY JOB. ANYTHING at all. BUT there are some rules... you MUST raise their hand, and no one can more than one question at a time...NO Question will go UNANSWERED. The person who can ask me the most questions in 3 minutes gets..."*

What do they get? Prize, product, or discount off their orders placed at the Party.

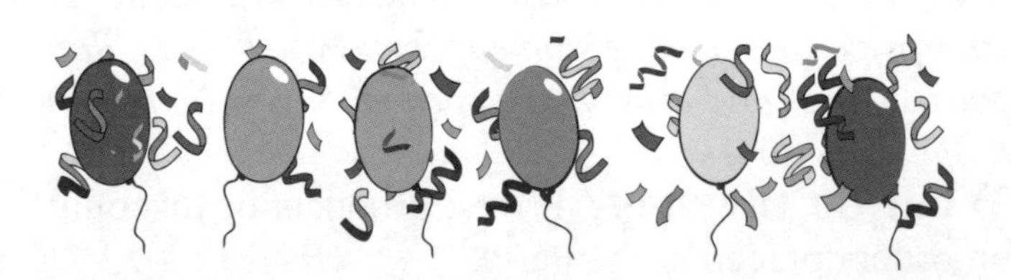

Christmas Fun

Explain the Game: Give each guest a sheet of paper and have the guests follow instructions. *"The idea is to draw a Santa with your eyes closed. Each part should connect if possible. No peeking!"*

What do they get? Guest with the most points gets a prize product or discount on their order.

Draw a circle (the body).
Draw a smaller circle (the head).
Draw his left leg.
Now draw his right arm.
Draw his nose on the head.
Draw his boot on his left leg.
Now draw his right leg.
He needs to see, so draw his eyes.
Now draw a sack beside Santa.
Now draw his beard.
Draw his boot on his right leg. Draw his left arm.
Now draw some presents in the sack.
Its very cold outside, Santa needs his gloves on his hands and a hat on his head.
(When reading these directions, just don't read them with a boring voice. Say things like: "Santa's left foot is cold, give him a boot" or "Santa needs a present to give-put one in his sack," etc.)

Points: Have them score themselves.
10 points if Santa's legs are in the right place.
15 points if Santa's nose is on his head.
20 points if Santa's boots are on his legs.
25 points if you put eyes on the head.
30 points for Santa's sack.
35 points if Santa's gloves are attached to his arms.
40 points if the presents are in his sack.
40 points for both arms attached.
50 points if Santa's beard is on his face.
75 points if Santa's hat is in its proper place.
Have everyone total their own points.

The Bingo Game #1

Explain the Game: *"We are going to play regular BINGO and the only difference is that the prizes are my products, not money. Please take my flyer and pass it to your friends as we will play Bingo again on (date.)"*

The Rules: Give a dollar value for each card.

Then start the game: This is real bingo. Keep it inexpensive and give away products. Just another way of getting your name out into the masses.

What do they get? A whole lot of fun. We will have a drawing for the money collected. The person who gets the money to invest in (company name) products.

The Bingo Game #2

Explain the Game: *"Please everyone pick a product to demonstrate."*

What do they get? Give a prize to each guest after they *"present"* their item. All guests that participated in the Party get to put their name in to the drawing and draw out a couple of names and give away free products. You can always break up a product into smaller items.

Prior to the Party:

1. Send invitations to your guests telling them that at your Party you are going to play a quick game of Bingo so that they can have a chance to win prizes. (Let guests know they will receive an additional bingo card for bringing a guest.)
2. At the Party you will give Bingo Cards for several different reasons. (1 for bringing a friend, 1 for coming on time, 1 for wearing red, etc.) Make your own bingo cards.
3. Give your products for prizes.

Hint: When playing bingo use paper cards that can be tossed away after you play the game.

Rules:

1. Each guest receives 1 bingo card for coming.
2. Each guest receives 1 bingo card for placing an order.
3. Each guest receives 2 bingo cards for a $25 order.
4. You can increase cards as sales increase.
5. Each guest receives 1 bingo card for bringing a guest. Play bingo!

What's Your Score Game

First: Give all guests a piece of paper and pen.

Explain the Game: *"I am going to read a quick story and want you to listen carefully and score yourself."*

What do they get? Prizes, free products or discount on orders placed at the Party.

STORY For Distributor to read:

If any selling you have done, put down 10 for the start of your score.

If you have a car, and are able to drive, the thing you must do is just add 5.

If some extra money is what you would like, add 10 more, which is just right.

A little spare time will add to your score, for this you may add 15 more.

If you like people and think they are grand, add 6 more to see where you stand.

Add 10 points if you think Parties are fun,
and when you add this, you are almost done.

If you score the highest, it is plain to see, that part of our (company name) successline you should be.

Add 25 to your score if you want to know more about becoming a distributor like me...learn how you can make money AND get (company benefits).

*guest's add up the points.

The Ticket Game

Prior to the Party: (Create tickets.)

Explain the Game: *"I have a ticket for you today at the Party because (different reasons at the Party; the person who arrives first; someone who brings a guest, etc.) I will soon pass out order forms, and kit request forms for those of you who would like to become a distributor and do what I am doing soon. Please complete the top portion of the form for a drawing I am going to hold after the Party."*

Next: During your presentation, ask guests to write down the name of five or more friends, and the first person finished gets a ticket for each friends name the write down in 2 minutes that they can think of who would be interested in your products. Do the same with neighbors, relatives, co-workers etc.

What do they get? Prizes, products or discount off their order place at the Party.

Benefit: The guests think they have played a fun game, but what they have really done, is fill out their guest list. When you ask them to schedule a Party and if they say they are not interested, ask them what they plan to do with their guest list. Can the guest next to them have it to use at their show? Of COURSE NOT! They usually will reconsider when they realize the hard part of making a list of *"who to invite"* is already done!

Betty Boop, Popeye And The Wolf Game

Explain the Game: *"Please divide yourselves into 3 smaller groups...called: Betty, Popeye and the Wolf. I am going to read you a quick story."*

Say: *"When I mention 'Betty' that group will stand up and say: 'Boop-Boop-De-Doo'. (with hip action) When I mention 'Popeye' that group stand up and say loudly: 'Well, blow me down' When I mention 'Wolf' that group stand up and give a 'Wolf Whistle'."*

Here is the story to read:

Once upon a time, there was a charming young lady named BETTY (Pause for group action each time you mention Betty, Popeye and Wolf) who was loved by a sailor called POPEYE. BETTY lived near a great forest in which there roamed a big WOLF. One day BETTY decided to visit her grandmother who lived in the heart of the forest where the WOLF lived, but BETTY would not listen and would not let POPEYE accompany her. Soon the WOLF followed BETTY, and he crept closer and closer. But, behind him came POPEYE! Just as the WOLF was about to leap on BETTY, POPEYE hit him with his trusty club and saved BETTY'S life. Thus the end of the story of POPEYE, BETTY BOOP and the Big Bad WOLF.

What do they get? Fun!

Success is in the preparation

The Blind Island Game

Explain the Game: *"Here is a sheet of paper and a pen. Please close your eyes and visualize that you are on an Island. You must keep eyes closed the entire game. You are going to get points for playing and the person with the most points at the end of the game will get a discount on their order. Here we go!"* (Don't tell them the scoring until after they have drawn the picture.)

On your paper, draw an Island. WHICH MUST BE IN THE MIDDLE OF THE PIECE OF PAPER. (10 points). Draw a sun in the sky IN THE RIGHT HAND CORNER (15), draw THREE OR MORE FISH in the sea (20), a palm tree on the island, which MUST BE IN THE MIDDLE OF THE ISLAND (25), draw a ship in the sea (30), draw THREE OR MORE birds in the sky (35), draw a hula girl TO THE RIGHT of the palm tree, (40), draw port holes on the ship (45), draw a tropical drink in the hula girl's hand THE DRINK HAS TO BE TOUCHING THE GIRL(50), and last but not least a sailor on the ship THE SAILOR MUST BE TOUCHING THE SHIP(55).

Benefit: Everyone has a lot of fun, gets to show their drawings and the one with the most points wins.

What do they get? Prize, Product, Discount on order placed at the Party.

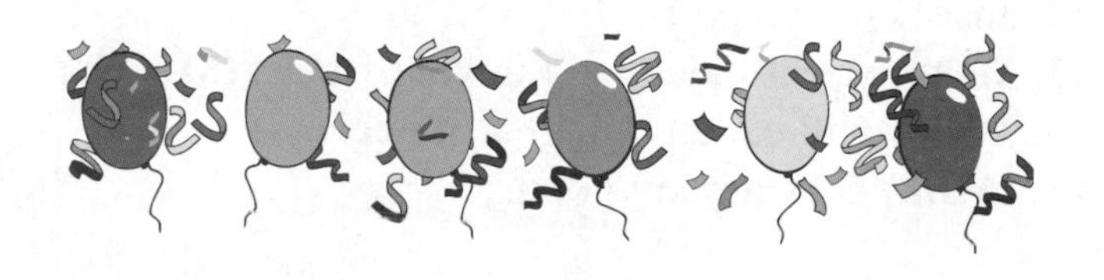

Let's Make A Deal Game

Take to the Party: Four envelopes and a basket with inexpensive door prizes. **Next:** Gift wrap all the items and put into the basket. **Next:** Inside each envelope, put a small piece of paper folded several times so guests cannot see it. On one, write $1; one will say $2: one will say $3 and one will say $5 (make up your own amounts.) Tell everyone what is inside the envelopes and that they are gift certificate towards their order at the Party only.

Explain the Game: *"The first guest to my left please choose and pick up one of the envelopes. Don't look inside of it! Now we are going to play a "Right-Left" game. The envelope will travel right and left. At the end to the game, the person will get the envelope and will have to make a decision at that time."*

Next: Play The Right-Left Game. When the envelope stops at the end of the game say to the guest: *"DON'T LOOK IN THE ENVELOPE! I want to 'Make A Deal' with you. You can trade for it for another envelope if you want to."* (Hold up the other envelopes.) Usually everyone is hollering '*Trade*' or *'Don't trade'*. Once the guests makes a choice...

Next say: *"DON'T LOOK! I'll make another deal with you...*(Pull out your gift basket) *I will trade you the envelope for an item in my basket...that envelope could be worth $5 or maybe just $1."* (Everyone is again yelling '*trade*' or '*don't trade*'). When they makes their choice...

Say: *"DON'T LOOK! I have another deal to make with you...I will give you your envelope back and DOUBLE what's inside or give you TWO prizes from my basket IF you will schedule a Home Party tonight in your home for your friends next two weeks."*

If they don't schedule a Party they get either what's in the envelope or the product out of the basket they choose. But MOST of the time they will schedule a Party with you. Play this at the end of your Party because by then they are already thinking about having a Party.

The Left Right Game

Prior to the Party: Gift wrap a present.

At the Party: Give the gift to the Host to hold and say to the guests: *"We are going to play quickly The Left-Right Game. Each time you hear the WORDS left or right pass the gift to the guest on your left or to the guest on your right. The one holding the gift in the end gets to keep it. I am going to read the story to you now:"* **Read:** I **left** the house **right** on time to get to (Host's) house. I had everything I needed to set up my display the **right** way, and place our wonderful products **right** before your eyes. My first turn was to the **right**, and then I turned **left**. Then I had to turn **right**, **right** again, and then **left**. I hoped that I remembered the **right** way to get to here. After I made the **lefts** and the **rights**, I found that my memory was **right** on target. I was **right** where I needed to be, here at (Host's) house. As I unloaded the car, I checked to make sure nothing was **left** behind. Putting one bag on my **left** shoulder and holding another with my **right** hand, I approached the door. Knocking with my **right** hand, I waited for (Host) to answer. After I set my samples down on the **left** of the room and my display items on the **right**, I was ready to start passing the samples. I say, *"Please sample these products on your left hand and arm."* As each item was introduced, I handed it to the person on my **right**, who passed it to the **right** and so on. Once you have sampled the high quality products, please open your catalogs **right** away. There are so many awesome products on each page... make sure you look on the **left** side AND the right so you don't miss a single one! I am going to begin passing around products to sample **right** now. Please feel free to ask me any questions you may have at any time. Now, let's congratulate the winner. She is patiently waiting to the **left** of whoever is holding the prize. I know you are all envious, because YOU wanted to win that prize, **right**? **RIGHT**!

Jingles

Explain the Game: *"I am going to read the following quotes and want you to try and figure out where the saying came from."*

What do they get? The one that guesses the most wins a prize, product or discount on their order at the Party.

1. Because I am worth it. **(L'Oreal)**
2. Nothing says Lovin like fresh from the Oven. **(Pillsbury)**
3. A little dab'll do ya. **(Brylcream)**
4. Get your kicks on. **(Route 66)**
5. You got the right one, baby. **(Diet Pepsi)**
6. The Real Thing, or Id like to teach the world to sing. **(Coca Cola)**
7. Good to the last drop. **(Maxwell House)**
8. Mountain Grown. **(Folgers)**
9. (**Winstons**) tastes good, like a cigarette should
10. Taste the rainbow. **(Skittles)**
11. Like sands in the hourglass, so are the **(Days of our Lives)**.
12. Just Do It. **(Nike)**
13. Melts in your mouth, not in your hands. **(M&Ms)**
14. Mikey will eat anything. **(Life cereal)**
15. **(Milk)** does a body good.

The Pass That Gift Game

Prior to the Party: Gift wrap a present.

At the Party: Introduce yourself, and ask everyone stand up and get into a circle.

Explain the Game: *"I am going to hand this gift to one guest and then I would like you to follow the directions. We are going to play a game and the last guest with the gift in hand wins it. This game is a really fun one to play!"* **Now Read:** You thought this gift was meant for you. But I have other items to show you too. The one with the gift please look around, and give it to the one with eyes of brown. (They pass the gift.) You think you are the lucky one, but let us all share in the fun! Look around with eyes discreet, and give it to the one with the smallest feet. (They pass the gift.) Your feet are tiny and very small. Now hand it to someone very tall. (They pass the gift.) Please, take your time and do not be harried. Give it to the one who is longest married. (They pass the gift.) You must be proud of your married life, now pass this on to the newest wife. (They pass the gift.) Of this parcel you are bereft, give it to the one on your left. (They pass the gift.) The largest earring I am looking for now, if you are wearing them, step up with a bow. (They pass the gift.) Now to the person with buttons big or small, any kind, the most you can find gets the gift at this time. (They pass the gift.) Now do not get cross and please do not fight, but pass it to the third guest on your right. (They pass the gift.) We should stop now, don't you agree? The gift is yours to open and see.

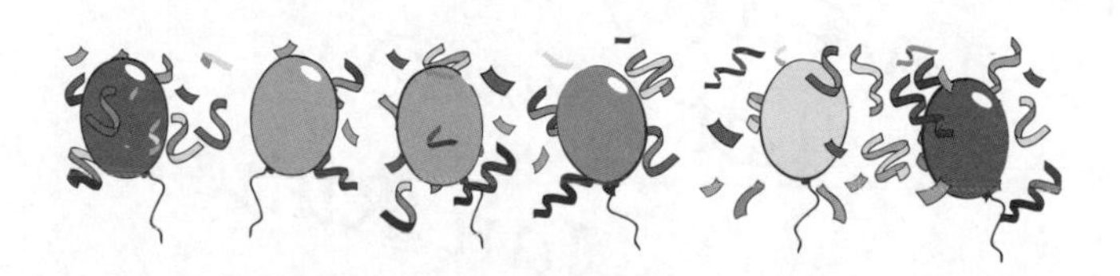

The Toilet Paper Game

Prior to the Party: Ask Host to call all guests two days before the Party and tell them to bring some toilet paper, never mind how much! This reminds Party guests about the Party, and makes them curious over why they are bringing TP! Take a large clear plastic bag to the Party.

Explain the Game: *"Did everyone bring their TP? Quickly, get it out and score yourself!"*

The award points are as follows:

Brought 10 sheets or less - 10 pts.
Brought more than 10 sheets, but not a roll - 20 pts.

Brought a roll - 30 pts.
Individually wrapped roll - 25 pts.
Brought a 4-pack - 50 pts.
Paper has: 1 ply - 15 pts.; 2 ply - 30 pts. 3 ply - 45 pts.
White paper - 50 pts.
Colored paper - 25 pts.
Designs or printed - 35 pts.
Brought on sale w/coupon - 20 pts.
Quilted - 50 pts.
Store/generic brand - 15 pts.
Name brand - 50 pts.
If you forgot to bring TP and borrowed some at Party - SUBTRACT 30 pts.

Next: Offer 100 points if they will give you their TP. After you collect all the TP offer 150 points to those who kept theirs.

What do they get? The guest with the most points gets a prize and give the bag of TP you just collected as an additional gag gift.

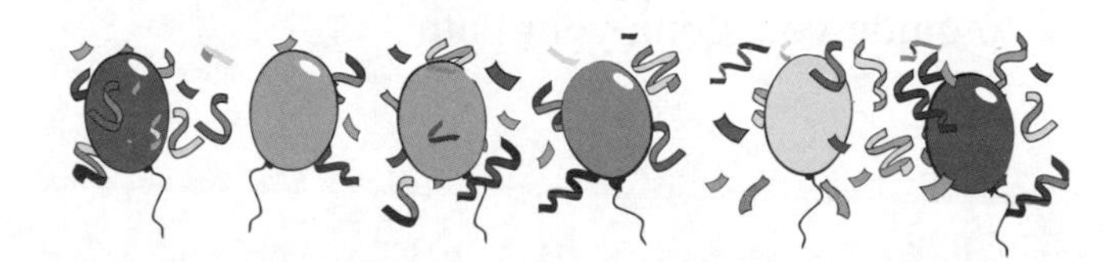

A Message From the Author

When I was writing *Let's Party*, it was my intention to deliver my message in as short a space as possible and not try to explain some of the techniques I used in depth. One reason was that I have written extensively about Network Marketing in my previously published books. Here are those references:

1. The Master Presentation Guide: I discuss the preparation and delivery for a presentation. There are over 1,000 opening lines for your Home Party presentations.
2. MLM Nuts $ Bolts: When you get a recruit at a Party you will want to be able to train your new recruit on how to succeed in Network Marketing. This is one of the premier books on Network Marketing worldwide.
3. The Lady of the Rings: This is a book for new recruits to help them learn the 10 most important concepts to master Network Marketing. An easy, quick, must read.
4. The Rhino Spirit: Having gone through some major upheavals in my life and business, I searched for quotes, poems and stories that would inspire me to continue to press onward in life. These are a collection of those stories that kept me going.
5. Fire Up!: This book will help you with your attitude and will help you keep a fired up spirit forever.
6. True Leadership: I co-authored this book with Art Burleigh, USA. We interviewed top leaders in Network Marketing and discovered their secrets. When you go into leadership, you will need this book to guide you along your path.
7. Go Diamond: I co-authored this book with Jayne Leach, UK. It's by 2 women, from across the Atlantic Ocean from each other, both single mothers who built their Network Marketing businesses in a similar way. We updated my original Duplicatable Training System that will help you train others to go to the top of your Pay Plan.

All of these books are available
online at www.janruhe.com
in the USA call 1-970-927-9380
or email BillRuhe@fireup.com

About the Author

Jan Ruhe with over 24 years of experience, has personally scheduled and held over 500 Home Parties. She has an organization that has held an astounding One MILLION Home Parties in her career. She invested $250 into a kit of products in 1980 and turned that investment into a multi-million dollar business. She was a single mother for 5 years, in debt over 6 figures, raised 3 children and built a powerful Network Marketing business. She blazed the trail and shares approaches that will help you to the top of Party Plan. Jan has trained over 100,000 distributors worldwide on how to get to the top of Network Marketing. Want to know what worked for her? Devour *Let's Party*!

Here is to your success in Party Plan .... "Let's Party!"

Jan Ruhe